T0147332

──────── Previous Books by the Author ────────

No Single Thread: Psychological Health in Family Systems,
   with W. Robert Beavers, John T. Gossett, and Virginia Austin Phillips

To Be A Therapist: The Teaching and Learning

How's Your Family?

Psychiatry in General Medical Practice,
   with Gene Usdin

The Family: Evaluation and Treatment,
   with Charles Hoffling

Treatment Planning in Psychiatry,
   with Gene Usdin

To Find A Way: The Outcome of Hospital Treatment of Disturbed Adolescents,
   with John T. Gossett and F. David Barnhart

The Long Struggle: Well-Functioning, Working-Class Black Families,
   with John Looney

The Birth of the Family: An Empirical Inquiry

Swimming Upstream: Teaching and Learning Psychotherapy in a Biological Era

The Monkey-Rope: A Psychotherapist's Reflections on Relationships

Marriage As A Search for Healing: Theory, Assessment, and Therapy

Disarming The Past: How an Intimate Relationship Can Heal Old Wounds,
   with John T. Gossett

Reflections on the Good Life: A Psychotherapist Writes to His Grandchildren

Famous Marriages: What They Can Teach Us

THE PSYCHOLOGY OF RELIGIOUS CALLINGS

A First Look

Jerry M. Lewis, M.D.

iUniverse, Inc.
New York   Bloomington

The Psychology of Religious Callings
A First Look

Copyright © 2009 by Jerry M. Lewis, M.D.

All rights reserved. No part of this book may be used or reproduced by any means, graphic, electronic, or mechanical, including photocopying, recording, taping or by any information storage retrieval system without the written permission of the publisher except in the case of brief quotations embodied in critical articles and reviews.

iUniverse books may be ordered through booksellers or by contacting:

iUniverse
1663 Liberty Drive
Bloomington, IN 47403
www.iuniverse.com
1-800-Authors (1-800-288-4677)

Because of the dynamic nature of the Internet, any Web addresses or links contained in this book may have changed since publication and may no longer be valid. The views expressed in this work are solely those of the author and do not necessarily reflect the views of the publisher, and the publisher hereby disclaims any responsibility for them.

ISBN: 978-1-4401-1762-6 (pbk)
ISBN: 978-1-4401-1763-3 (ebk)

Library of Congress Control Number: 2009922646

Printed in the United States of America

iUniverse rev. date: 6/25/09

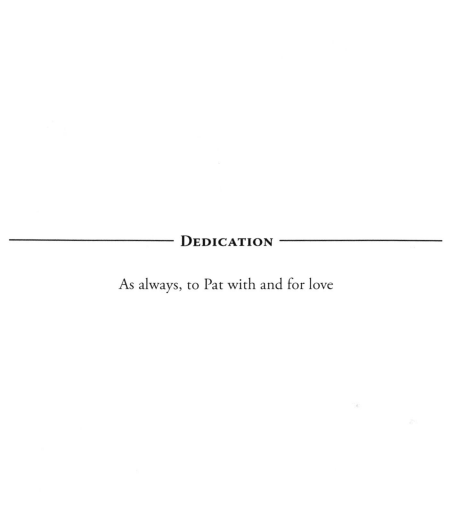

DEDICATION

As always, to Pat with and for love

Table of Contents

Acknowledgements

One writes a book alone yet in a context of others who encourage, question, and critique. This book is no exception and I trust that those in my close circle of family and friends know the crucial role they have played. Velma Byford has been the operational hub of transforming my writing in pencil to the printed page and has my ongoing gratitude.

PREFACE

It is, perhaps, of no surprise that this book is self-published. The lack of interest in the psychology of callings is emphasized in the initial chapter of this book and the same disinterest has been exhibited by those who publish at the interface of religion and psychology. "Too academic" some have written, and others have implied that there is little interest in the subject of callings. A friend and former editor in the area of psychology-psychiatry responded to the manuscript by writing "fascinating but a very hard sell." And so, the decision to self-publish is in itself a statement that I believe callings may be important adult psychological growth experiences and need more systematic attention. The reader will have to decide whether such is so.

CHAPTER 1

At The Beginning

It is hard to believe that there are life experiences more impactful than a call to a religious vocation. The conviction that God beckons one to His ministry changes the course of the person's life, often in dramatic ways. Those changes are frequently described in ways that suggest maturation of the personality, a new-found integration of previously disconnected or conflicted parts of the self. Thus, one would think that psychologists and psychiatrists interested in personality development would have studied such questions as "Who gets called?" "Under what circumstances do callings occur?" and "What are the consequences of being called?"

Such proves not to be the case. There are no systematic studies of the psychology of callings. The absence of such studies is all the more peculiar in light of the psychological studies of conversion that go back over 100 years to the seminal work of William James (1). If conversions have attracted the attention of scientists for so long, why not callings? This question will be addressed shortly but first a brief account of how this psychiatrist got involved with callings.

In 1995 I was asked to evaluate the psychological status of men and women aspiring to the priesthood or diaconate in the Episcopal Church. Although later this opportunity will be described in greater detail, for these introductory purposes I have now spent two to three hours interviewing each of 108 such persons. My primary task was to screen these individuals for psychological or mental health problems that could interfere with their functioning in these religious vocations. As one part of the interview process I asked them to describe their calling experiences. I did so not out of an interest in the theological aspects of their callings, rather because I believed that understanding the psychological context in which their callings were experienced would help me to better understand who they were psychologically.

At some point, perhaps after the first several dozen evaluations, I came to hear several themes. The themes are better described as developmental trajectories – the flow of their lives in which the callings took form. One group, mostly young adults, described their callings as occurring during the course of healthy development in loving, supportive, and usually religious families. There was not much pain or struggle in these calling stories; rather life had been good to these fortunate and well functioning young adults.

There were two other developmental pathways, and they were very different from the first group. Mostly middle-aged, these men and women described growing up in dysfunctional families (often involving abuse and/or neglect), leaving such families in late adolescence, and mostly successful college and vocational experiences. They also described usually multiple relationship failures. In sum, these aspirants were good at work but unsuccessful in love. One of the two groups described a life-transforming new relationship usually leading to a supportive marriage. It was in the context of some years of such a healing marriage that their call was gradually experienced and supported by their spouse.

The second of these two groups did not describe a healing marriage; rather their callings were described as growing out of the emergence from a crisis, often a severe depression. For a few of this group the concept of crisis is not correct in that what was described was several or more years of uncertainty and distress about the direction their lives had taken. These subjects were dissatisfied with their vocations, had perhaps made several changes, and were clearly searching for a new direction. Their callings provided that direction and relieved their distress. Although a large number of both the crisis and searcher groups received helpful psychiatric treatment (psychotherapy and psychotropic drugs), the experience of recovery was felt to be primarily a spiritual process. Thus, this group's calling appeared to involve a new and more meaningful relationship with God growing out of emergence from uncertainty, pain, and struggle.

These three groups – the fortunate-healthy, the healing marriage, and the crisis-searcher – are found to differ in other ways. These differences will be described in much of what follows in this book. There is, however, another important finding emerging from these calling narratives. Callings appear to re-enforce (in the healthy-fortunate) or to promote psychological maturation (in the healing marriage and crisis-searcher groups). Although I believe experienced clinicians can reliably identify current levels of psychological health, understanding positive changes from subjects' retrospective accounts is tricky business. Despite this difficulty it seems likely that for many of the aspirants the calling and a period of psychological maturation were intertwined. This conclusion and its implications will also occupy many of the pages that are to follow.

The essence of this book, then, is to report observations regarding certain psychological aspects of callings. This contribution is a product of qualitative research, and as such may lead to focused efforts to study callings in quantitative ways. I believe the absence of published psychological research on callings increases the importance of this qualitative study, not only to the religious community but also to mental health professionals wishing to better understand the many ways that adults may come to attain more mature levels of psychological health.

Before describing examples of calling stories it seems best to address the problems involved in studying callings as they are probably responsible for the absence of such studies.

Callings — A Slippery Concept

There is no widespread agreement on just what a calling is. Although most theologians may agree that a calling to a religious vocation is a message from God – that it originates outside the person experiencing the call, this distinction does not hold when the definition of callings is extended to other professions. Some persons feel called to medicine, the law, or other endeavors. Rarely do such persons believe their callings are divinely inspired. Rather, their origin is within the experienced self. So, the first ambiguity is regarding the source of a call. Dictionaries most often locate the source as inside the person: "a strong conviction, impulse, or propensity to a certain course of action" or something similar is usually given.

Psychologists and psychiatrists who try to bring scientific rigor to the study of human experience would likely not be troubled by this inside-outside dilemma for their assumption would be that, from a psychological perspective, callings have to originate within the person. Ascribing a calling to an outside agency would be understood as a type of secondary psychological process in the adaptive service of resolving doubt and conflict about a life-changing decision. The origin of a calling is a consequential issue psychologically in that it speaks to the activity-passivity dimension of personality. To experience the calling as an inner conviction and then act on it is in the service of taking charge of one's life, that which has been called efficacy. It is understood, at least in Western culture, as a personality strength. To experience oneself as responsive to a divine call is a more passive psychological position. Although stating the distinction in such absolute, either-or terms exaggerates the distinction, it seems to me that however both efficacy and responsiveness are involved, the balance may differ from person to person, and it is an important issue to keep in mind.

Another source of conceptual fuzziness about callings is the difficulty many find in putting spiritual experiences into words. This ineffable quality of spiritual and religious experiences has been noted for over one hundred years, and it continues to haunt efforts to study the psychology of callings. It would, for example, make understanding callings much easier if those called went through a series of identifiable cognitive phases. One such scenario might be:

1. I have thought about being a priest.
2. I have imagined myself as a priest.
3. I have wanted to be a priest.
4. I have decided to become a priest.
5. I have come to the conclusion that being a priest is who I am meant to be.
6. I have been called to being a priest.

This orderly progression (or something like it) from thought to fantasy, to wish, to decision, to imperative, to call might actually happen but, if so, it does not jump out at one when listening to persons' stories of being called. Perhaps if I had focused more specifically on such presumed cognitive structures some evidence might have emerged, but I did not. Indeed, the calling stories I heard usually involved a gradual process – often of several or more years of inner exploration, doubt, and excitement. Rarely is there anything very dramatic. Describing one's call can be difficult both because describing spiritual experiences is difficult and because the calling process is more often incremental than dramatic in its progression.

Calling stories involve the narration of past experiences, present circumstances, and anticipated futures. They are a subset of autobiographical narratives and, as such, present an interpretive dilemma. How are such stories to be understood? Entirely factual, part fiction or some individual combination of both? This is not to suggest that those called to religious vocations would lie about their experiences: rather, that the experience of being called may alter the recall of the past without one knowing it. This premise (the present influences the past just as the past influences the present) is at the heart of the narrative theory of personality and will be discussed in more detail in a later section of this book. It is noted here at the beginning because it contributes to the difficulty in understanding callings.

Another issue making the study of callings difficult is that of denominational differences. To be called to the priesthood or diaconate in the Episcopal Church is almost certainly a different psychological experience than being called to an evangelical Bible church ministry. The former requires years of study and fulfilling other pre-ordination requirements. The latter may involve only testimony without prescribed educational and experiential requirements. Although there are no psychological studies of such crucial denominational issues, it seems hardly possible not to postulate very different psychological processes at work. So, the qualitative data presented here about callings to ordination in the Episcopal Church reflect the narratives of only a small percentage of all those called to religious vocations. How generalizable they are to other denominations is still an open question.

There are other issues that make difficult broad agreement on the essential nature of callings. One is the relationship of callings to conversions. For some they are very different processes; for others callings contain elements of conversion. Once again psychologists would try to understand both callings and conversions as adaptive efforts. These efforts could have multiple goals – all the way from relieving doubt, conflict, and anxiety to finding greater meaning in life. Such studies (contrasting the two processes psychologically) have not been done, but my assumption is that most psychological hypotheses would postulate significant differences between adopting a new belief system (conversion) and becoming a special representative of God (calling).

Another necessary distinction is that between callings and careers. Bellah and his colleagues have done the most to clarify this issue (2). Careers are vocations that provide the individual with a sense of competence, success, and recognition. A career is thus something one does and, when successful, brings the sort of rewards noted. Callings are more apt to become part of who one is, to be assimilated into the basic sense of self. Both conversions and callings, therefore, are apt to change people. The changes are those that often suggest both personal maturation and societal approval.

Calling Stories

Until recently I believed that a start could be made in understanding the psychology of callings by focusing only on the narratives of those subjects whose response to their callings had been successful action. That is, they had converted their experienced call into life-changing behaviors the purpose of which was ordination as priest or deacon. I have come to believe that, however central such persons' calling narratives are to a beginning understanding of the psychology of callings, there are other types of calling stories that may help in that understanding. Here I refer to unfulfilled callings, unwanted callings, and projected callings. More about what may be learned from such stories later. A sense of the types of successful callings heard from the aspirants interviewed may be gained from these necessarily brief vignettes.

She was 43, a second year student at a local seminary and pursuing the Episcopal priesthood when we met for four semistructured interviews mandated by her diocese to evaluate her psychological suitability for a religious vocation.

Carol, as I will call her, was attractive and poised. She maintained eye contact and directly addressed a variety of unfortunate life experiences, often expressing openly the associated painful feelings. A brief summary of her life story starts with her being the oldest of six children of a violent, alcoholic factory worker and a chronically depressed mother. Her father was physically abusive to her mother and the children. She described violent beatings with closed fists and leather straps. Carol's response was to retreat emotionally and to comply behaviorally.

Carol did well in school, was something of a loner, and, after graduating from high school, moved to a distant city. She supported herself as a clerk in an insurance office and took college courses at night. She did well at her job and during the following seven years received many promotions. She also finished her college degree in accounting, and, at the time of her evaluation interviews had become the chief financial officer of the company for which she worked.

Carol's success at work was not matched in love. She entered a series of relationships with emotionally remote and unavailable men. Her first marriage was to a fellow worker who came to abuse her both verbally and physically. She had one child, a daughter, with this man. She left this marriage after her then husband began abusing their daughter, and remained single and uninvolved romantically for the next ten years. Four years before her evaluation she met and fell in love with a widowed man 12 years her senior. They married after a year of steady dating, and Carol described her second marriage as a major turning point in her life. "Don," she reported, "is the nicest man in the world. He is kind, loving, and very reliable. I have learned from him to trust, to be close – even vulnerable. He's a wonderful father to my daughter, and she adores him. I really didn't believe that there were men like Don: in fact at some level within me I felt all men were dangerous. He and his love have really changed who I am. I'm much more open, affectionate, and at peace with myself than I've ever been before."

Carol's religious involvements started early in her life. When she was 12 she went by herself to a nearby fundamentalist Bible church where in the youth group she found a sense of acceptance and safety. "That youth group and its minister were a real haven for me" she recalled tearfully. After her first marriage failed, she searched for a new church home and was strongly attracted to an Episcopal congregation and its rector. She became an active participant, often in leadership roles.

When asked to describe her calling to the priesthood, she said, "My calling is hard to describe. It started after I married Don and began to know what it's like to really feel loved. At first it was sort of a yearning to do more for others. Then one Sunday at services I had an intense experience, a sense of peace and oneness, a feeling that God might be calling me. I talked about it with Don and he encouraged me to discuss it with our rector. I did, and he blew me away by saying that he had anticipated my coming to him – that I would be called to the priesthood. Further, he told me that he would support me if I decided to respond to this calling. And that's how it all got started – and I'm still kind of shocked about it but, most of all, I am deeply convinced that this is what God intends for me to do."

Carol's calling narrative – although much abbreviated here – illustrates a process involving both a strong inner conviction and the belief that she is responding to a message from God. The details of her psychological pathway to a calling centered about her marriage to Don, a healing relationship. More about that pattern will be described later.

Jim is a 26 year old single man engaged to his college girlfriend and about to begin seminary. His life story begins with the good fortune of having been born into a loving family. He describes his parents as "solid, supportive, and loving." He is the younger of two children, and his sister, three years his senior, is in her final year of medical school. "We have always been a close family," he said, "and our parents encouraged both of us to get as much education as possible. They had not been able to do so and ended up in midlevel white collar jobs. Money was usually pretty tight. Most of all, though, they love each other and it is obvious. They spent a lot of time with my sister and me, encouraging us to be whatever we wanted to be. My sister started out as a nursing student but after a year or so switched to premed. Now she's almost a doctor! I wasn't sure about what I wanted to be when I started college – kind of played with the idea of going to law school. But one Sunday I went to Episcopal services with my roommate and had – I guess you'd call it a spiritual experience. No voices or visions – just a feeling of peace and wanting to be a part of it somehow. I told my parents about it, and they wondered if it might be the beginning of a calling. They're religious and church activities were a big part of my growing up. They're not Episcopalians, and early on were members of a Bible church but switched to the Methodist Church when I was very young. When I told them about my experience in the Episcopal Church they encouraged me to continue attending. I did so for more than a year and then began meeting with the rector. She encouraged me to keep myself open to the possibility that I was being called. After I graduated I went into the Peace Corps for two years – went to the very southern part of Mexico and worked in several villages helping to improve their sanitation systems. During those two years my sense of being called to the priesthood solidified. When I got back I spent more time with my rector and started the process leading to ordination."

His girlfriend is in graduate school, and they hope to marry when she finishes her studies and begins a career as a teacher. She is reported to be very supportive of his calling.

Jim's life story is one of the good fortunes of his birth and subsequent healthy psychological development. He has not experienced any anxiety other than that which is situation-based. There is no history of depressive episodes or other psychological symptoms. In our interviews he was thoughtful, direct, and with an engaging manner. He clearly seemed to be functioning at a healthy psychological level.

Jim's calling narrative is a pattern of good fortune and healthy psychological development. It can be understood as growing out of his experiences in a healthy family of origin (FOO) and identification with that family's strong religious belief system. It is another psychological pattern associated with some persons' callings. We will return in detail to this pattern in subsequent parts of this book.

> Laurence is a 56 year old attorney whose calling to the Episcopal diaconate appears to have evolved as part of a struggle to overcome a major depressive disorder some years earlier. When he was in his early 40s his wife left him and their two children for another man. Although a successful partner in a small law firm with a circle of friends and a major investment in parenting his two sons, he was devastated by his wife's affair and leaving the family. "I was" he said, "absolutely immobilized – couldn't go to work, felt both terribly sad and very agitated, quit eating and lost 30 pounds. Wasn't sleeping, thought of ending it all and might have if it weren't for my sons. I began working with a psychiatrist and taking antidepressants. Over a period of a year or so I began to get on top of it. The therapy and medicine helped a great deal but most of all it felt like my recovery was spiritual – that God, prayer, and my priest were all essential to my coming out of that depression."
>
> Laurence described growing up in a family that did not express feelings openly. "My parents were good people but loners. I have no memories of affection – no hugs or kisses. I sort of knew they loved me, but I grew up a stranger to open affection. Not surprisingly, I turned out to be an emotional distancer myself, and that's probably one of the reasons my wife left me. I have always been pretty compliant, an achiever of sorts. Thought of myself as a good provider and had absolutely no sense of how unavailable I was. The depression changed all of that."
>
> Laurence's recovery from his major depression and the spiritual aspects of his experienced recovery led to increasing involvement in his parish church. "Ultimately, I came to function as if I was a deacon, and five or six years ago began to wonder about seeking ordination. Began to talk with my rector,

and he encouraged me. I'm taking some required courses and am excited about the future."

Laurence's calling narrative is very different from those of Carol and Jim. It does however illustrate yet another pattern involving the emergence from a crisis and is heard from some of the interviewed aspirants. I will also return to this pattern in later sections of this book.

Ruth, a 37 year old masters level psychotherapist, was pursuing the priesthood and was in her third year of part-time study at a local seminary. She continued to support herself and her 12 year-old daughter by working as a therapist in a group led by a psychiatrist.

Ruth described her childhood as difficult in that neither of her parents were openly affectionate with her and gave no evidence of liking each other. "Emotionally," she reflected, "it was like growing up in a sterile abscess. It's a wonder I didn't turn out to be oppositional or even antisocial. But, I kept trying to please them – good grades and all the rest. Went to a junior college first and, not surprisingly, got very interested in psychology. I entered therapy there in student health and that was helpful. Got an undergraduate degree in social work and an academic scholarship to get my masters. Married a fellow graduate student who turned out to be as unavailable as my parents were. We did have Amy before we divorced and she is a blessing."

When asked about her calling to the priesthood, she responded. "It has been gradual. All my adult life I've felt there was something missing – and I have looked everywhere for it. Solo private practice, three different social agencies, and now the group I am in. I've always found support in my church and been active, often in a leadership role. Several years ago I began to feel more and more at peace during services – the sacraments particularly give me something I've never had before. Not sure how to describe it – peace, more connected to God – something different than ever before. Finally talked with my rector, and we began meeting. He said he thought I was being called. Clearly its going to take a lot of time, but it really feels right."

Ruth had not really experienced a crisis and no diagnosable psychiatric syndrome. She is an example of those whose calling appears to have emerged from years of searching for who she was and who she was suppose to be.

Carol, Jim, Laurence, and Ruth's calling narratives illustrate the four types heard (with very few exceptions) from those persons actively involved in seeking ordination in the Episcopal Church. Although they have many more steps to accomplish, they can be considered launched in their calling and, from that perspective, successful. Whether they will all be ordained is yet to be seen. What, though, about others whose experienced callings seemed to have originated in the minds of others or have not resulted in an active pursuit? Brief illustrations may help.

Projected Callings

Family projection systems may be ubiquitous and only harmful if they mandate a narrow identity for the developing child. There is a vast difference in receiving subtle messages from a parent that encourage a child to find his or her vocation and work hard to prepare for it and receiving messages that say "you must be a priest, doctor, or whatever." In the latter instance there is often the implicit threat of withdrawal of affection if the projection is not affirmed. In the middle class apartment neighborhood of Chicago where I spent much of my childhood we sensed at age 9 or 10 that certain of our playmates were going to be nuns, priests, or rabbis. They had to be responding to parental projections for in their Irish Catholic and Jewish families having a child follow a religious vocation was usually highly prized and a marker of parental success.

I did not find evidence of such projection systems in the persons interviewed, but that may not be surprising. First, such projections often operate out of consciousness and/or may have been edited out in the ongoing re-construction of an autobiographical identity. Also it is hardly a wise tactic to describe one's calling as responding to a parent's need or wish. Family projections are described, however, in psychotherapy sessions often with depressed professionals during midlife.

Jack, for example, an Episcopal priest was referred by his Canon for treatment of depression. I saw him twice monthly in psychotherapy (he came from over 100 miles away) and prescribed an antidepressant. His depression gradually disappeared over the course of the year I saw him. At the beginning he was filled with doubt about his marriage, his effectiveness as a priest, and about most aspects of his life. There is much that could be said about him but for present purposes I shall focus only on his reflections of his decision to become a priest. He said that he decided during adolescence to pursue the ordained ministry and was not at all sure about his call. "My mother was very religious – at church whenever the doors were unlocked. She was basically unhappy with my father and long-suffering. She was also almost always sick, probably a severe hypochondriac. Not surprisingly my older brother went into medicine where he has not been particularly happy. As the younger son I knew she wanted me to become a minister, not particularly an Episcopal priest, rather a Baptist preacher – her church. She never actually said that I must become a minister, but it was there, kind of hanging in the space between us. I think becoming a priest was in part the need to please her, to try and make her happy and well. Choosing a different denomination than hers was my stab at some degree of self-determination. She did become proud of me, I think. Her two sons entered the fields that her life was all about – sickness and God. So, I'm not sure that feeling called was as much my own as it is for most others."

This man was, I thought, when not depressed a competent priest who truly cared about those he ministered to. He had no driving ambition beyond being a rector in a small parish, and when his depression relented he regained his enthusiasm for his pastoral duties. His recollections of his calling do suggest that his calling was at least in part a projection from his mother of her needs. He was insightful about this family dynamic but had overcome it to the extent that he enjoyed and found meaning in his priestly vocation.

Unfulfilled Callings

There are those who report early life experiences that suggest callings, but something appears to have interfered and the calling was not following by action. I have known persons who described unfulfilled callings – some as friends and some as psychotherapy patients.

"Where are your diplomas?" he asked mildly as he looked around my office. "They're at home," I responded matter-of-factly. "Why do you ask?" "I wanted so much to be a doctor, really felt called to medicine until I was almost 30," he said with clear sadness. "What happened?" I said softly. "I couldn't do any better than a C in organic chemistry. Took it several times but always with the same result. Medical schools won't admit you with a C in organic. At least they wouldn't admit me."

Harold was a sad middle-aged man, a successful sales executive, who was referred because of recurring depressed periods. Further explorations revealed that his story of an unfulfilled calling to be a doctor, while important in its own right, was also a reflection of a larger life theme – that of things not working out, of disappointments, and self-blame. His economic success had not brought much satisfaction. His stable marriage was somehow not enough, and he felt responsible. His two children were doing well (one, perhaps unsurprisingly, in premed studies) but he took no credit, felt no pride. Although this major life theme seemed apparent, I wondered where it came from. His description of his childhood contained no obvious clues. It was only when we returned to his calling that I began to suspect that the unfulfilled outcome had been formative, the very beginning of what was to become his inability to experience himself as successful. His calling to medicine began when he was nine years old. There were several factors that appeared to be involved. His maternal grandfather was a respected general practitioner in the small town where he grew up. His mother idolized her father and his gentle, compassionate manner. The grandfather never explicitly encouraged my patient to follow his footsteps, but was a readily available figure with whom to identify. There were also several dramatic events he experienced at age 12 that involved life-saving interventions by physicians in extended family members. These were much talked-about in his family, and the physicians were openly admired.

He also was good at math and science and encouraged by teachers to consider becoming a doctor "like his grandfather." And so he gradually came to believe that he was meant to be a doctor. It was, he said, more than a wish, rather a "sort-of inner conviction."

His later inability to make a high enough grade in college organic chemistry is something of a mystery. Most premed students know that they must do well in that course and whatever their natural affinity for chemistry study long and hard enough to do so. Many years ago I was one of those without interest in or affinity for chemistry who knew that organic chemistry was part of the game one had to play to get into medical school. It took an inordinate amount of time studying (mostly memorizing things I really didn't understand in any fundamental way) and the same was true of many of my premed classmates. This required a good deal of self-discipline for most nights there were far more pleasant activities beckoning. Why had my obviously bright patient not done what was necessary to get higher grades in organic chemistry? I never found out because after a few sessions he stopped coming (psychotherapy as yet another disappointment?). The reasons for his failure to do what was necessary to actuate his calling remain a mystery.

Harold's unfulfilled calling narrative illustrates that however intensely a calling may be experienced, action is required. Harold did not do what was required to activate his calling, and his story illustrates both that callings require work — usually years of some degree of self-deprivation — and that the failure to successfully pursue a calling may shape important aspects of one's future self.

I have known others whose unfulfilled callings seemed less a personal failure to activate the inner conviction but more the outcome of circumstances beyond the individual's control. I once worked with a man who talked with me about his calling to medicine and going to medical school for one year and dropping out during the depression because he had to find work, in part to support his parents. Why he never made efforts to return to his calling was never explored. His sadness 40 years later about not being a doctor was obvious, and in our conversation he quickly moved away from the topic. If, however, you take his story at face value his economic circumstances were the primary reasons for his unfulfilled calling.

Resisted Callings

There is another type of calling experience that may help our understanding of the calling phenomena more generally. This type can be thought of as resisted callings, that is when the inner conviction is actively resisted. An illustration of this perhaps rare circumstance is presented by Wendell Berry in his novel Jayber Crow (3).

> Jayber is the town barber in Berry's fictional town of Port William, Kentucky, and this novel concerns his recollections of his life at age 72. His early life was dominated by loss. His parents died when he was four and he went to live with his great aunt and uncle who died when he was ten. He was then placed in an orphanage run by religious fundamentalists where Jayber had few relationships and was clearly withdrawn and lonely. In his early teens he began to be sexually attracted to several of the girls in the orphanage and this was frightening to him. Thus this was the developmental context in which Jayber experienced his calling.
>
> "How it came about I am not quite sure, but I began to suspect that I might be called to preach. My suspicion may have been no more than fear, for with all my heart I disliked the idea of becoming a preacher" (3, p. 42).
>
> "My fearful uncertainty lasted for months. As the siren song of girls became even stronger in my mind, I wondered if maybe that was the trouble. Finally I reasoned that in dealing with God you had better give Him the benefit of the doubt. I decided that I had better accept the call that had not come, just in case it had come and I had missed it" (3, p. 43).
>
> Jayber discloses his call to the religious leader of the orphanage and, not surprisingly, becomes very special in that

setting, receiving a scholarship to a small denominational college as a preministerial student. He pursues that course for several years until his doubt is transformed to the conviction that he is moving in the wrong direction and with the support of a professor he drops out.

Jayber may or may not have been called but his calling experience underscores both that callings have developmental contexts and that dealing with inner doubt and conflict may be an important part of the calling experience.

I experienced what I recall as a call to medicine as a teenager and will describe it now as the final illustration of several of the psychological dynamics of calling experiences.

My Calling to Medicine

At age 16 or 17, I developed an inner conviction that I should be a doctor. It was strong belief and was experienced in a certain psychological context. First of all, late adolescence and early adulthood are the developmental phases in which one's identity begin to crystallize. Under the best of circumstances one starts to address the questions of "Who am I?" and "Who do I want to be?" Up until that time I hoped to play professional baseball, but good curve-ball pitchers had begun to erode the possibility of that dream. I did not feel called to baseball; rather just thought doing so would be a wonderful way to spend one's life doing something so intrinsically pleasurable. My calling to medicine was very different; becoming a doctor was something I was meant to be.

I have written above, that during mid-adolescence I developed the conviction that I should be a doctor. Although that is my memory, it almost certainly is an oversimplification. Convictions, I believe, rarely arise de novo. In an earlier section I have suggested the possibility of a sequence of cognitive stages and that was my experience. First there is interest in the vocation. My interest in medicine was likely stimulated by our family doctor's care of my badly burned younger sister. He came to our home each day, and was clearly esteemed by my parents. I was eight years old at the time, and a few years later first asked myself if I could be a doctor. Out of the internal processes of interest and questioning came a third process – desire. I became gradually aware that I wanted to be a doctor. Although I have no systematic data on such a progression of internal states, these three overlapping processes can be understood as setting the stage for the final subjective state, that of conviction. It is likely that the stage of conviction (the calling) is not experienced by most persons seeking a professional vocation. Their motivation most often springs from the desire or wish.

To return to my adolescent experience, my sense of conviction occurred in a certain context. This context (aside from the developmental issue) involved my parents and primarily my father. He had been a poor farm boy and at an early age left home to join the army in the border skirmish with Mexico. He quickly rose to a noncommissioned officer status and when his cavalry division was sent to Europe to fight in World War I, he was selected to go to the French version of West Point and become an officer. He loved being an officer. It provided upward social mobility for a poor boy. He was much decorated and, after the war, distressed when in his division's downsizing only officers who were graduates of our military academy at West Point were retained. Although he subsequently had a successful business career, his continuing wish was to have risen to command levels as an Army officer. It is, perhaps, no surprise that he wanted me to fulfill his dream, obtained for me the promise of a congressional appointment to West Point, and was unenthusiastic about my desire to be a doctor. Thus, my calling to medicine arose in an appropriate developmental stage but also in the context of a mostly unspoken conflict about who was to be in charge of my identity. My autonomy was the issue, and it was not easy to resolve for my father was a powerful, charismatic man. I flunked the then rigorous visual examination and that provided a resolution of sorts. He remained ambivalent about my calling to medicine – often stating that one needed to get out and make a living as quickly as possible.

To take an oppositional stance to a powerful parent is difficult and the help of an influential other is often necessary. My mother provided this. She had a romanticized view of doctors (Paul Muni, an early movie actor, played a doctor in a popular film of those days and often wore a white linen suit. Guess what she gave me when I graduated from medical school!) Regardless of her romantic notions, she played a mostly subtle role encouraging me to oppose my father, and psychologically I needed her support.

My interpretation of my calling involves emphasizing the pursuit of a higher level of autonomy, one piece of psychological growth during late adolescence and throughout adulthood. Whether this calling experience to medicine represents the facilitation of my psychological growth is impossible for me to determine in any objective way.

Before summarizing what I believe these calling stories suggest about the psychology of callings, there are some useful insights available in those persons who have written about callings. Although there is no systematic psychological research, several writers and social scientists have speculated about callings in helpful ways.

Insights From The Literature

The work of Bellah and his colleagues has been mentioned earlier (2). They offer the helpful idea that callings differ from careers in that they become part of who one is. "In a calling . . . . one gives oneself to learning and practicing activities that in turn define the self and enter into the shape of its character" (2, p. 69). Thus, Bellah speaks to the effects of the calling experience. One is changed and the basic sense of self comes to include that which one has been called to do.

Baumeister, a leading student of meanings in life, also addresses callings as linked to the quest for self-actualization (4). Unlike jobs and careers, callings are inherently effective means of satisfying the need for value (endowed with a powerful sense of being right, good, necessary, and involving hardships and sacrifices). Callings may also promise fulfillment as part of one's destiny. "Thus", Baumeister writes, "callings emphasize the two needs for meaning that are most problematic in modern life: value and fulfillment" (4, p. 127). He also suggests that callings can be combined with career attitudes in many professionals with the calling component providing value and fulfillment and the career component bringing achievement, recognition, and success. In making this suggestion Baumeister is taking the position that callings and careers (although not, it seems, jobs) are not mutually exclusive. Perhaps, as Bellah writes, it is helpful to think of callings as impacting on the basic sense of self (who one is) and career as activities that bring something positive to the self (what one has accomplished).

The writer, Minna Proctor, has written a fine book on callings in general and, in particular, the discernment process in the Episcopal Church in which committees evaluate the nature of an individual's calling (5). The impetus for her contribution was a discernment committee's refusal to validate her father's later life calling. Proctor's thinking about callings is broad and complex. She reviews the history of the idea of a calling, beginning, she believes with the Israelites and moving through history to its present state – one in which it has lost its ideational specificity and in common usage has become vague and fluid, "a word we use instinctively to define something vaguely that we feel specifically" (5, p. 77). Although callings involve the sense that one is involved in a worthy vocation, that attitude is often difficult to maintain on a daily basis. The experience of a calling is not usually a moment of revelation, rather a summons that is gradual, often unspecific, and closer to a yearning than anything else. The experience of feeling called is described as a story, and, although each person's calling may differ from others, there are common elements. The mystics, she writes, experience God "tapping you on the shoulder, appearing in a vision, weeping in your ear. The emotionalists experience a sense of anguish and restlessness resulting in collapse and then great peace. Empiricists feel their way into their callings" (5, p. 103). Thus, Proctor suggests a beginning taxonomy of calling based on personality factors. She also suggests underlying dynamics in the form of either seeking penance for past mistakes or mitigating dissatisfaction with one's present circumstances. For some, perhaps many, there is the sense of being at a crossroad in life – one that will define the future.

Proctor approaches the consequences of a calling with much caution. She quotes an early 19th century sermon by Newman in which he proposed that callings can result in moving from a lower region to a higher one, of changes not as great as to entirely reverse former opinions and conduct but as being able to see new connections. In current psychological language this seems to suggest a higher level of personality integration, perhaps a greater capacity for tolerating internal contradictions.

Proctor also suggests the risks of acknowledging one's calling to others, including the church's hierarchy. One needs affirmation of a calling yet risks rejection. Thus, she speaks to that part of the calling that is relational.

I have summarized Proctor's ideas liberally because she focuses on many of the relevant issues that need addressing if one hopes to begin the process of a psychological inquiry into the nature of callings.

An Emerging Psychological Model

I wish to emphasize that the attempt to understand the psychology of callings is not meant to detract from the theological implications of callings. Those who focus entirely on the theology of callings may have to entertain the idea that looking at callings psychologically is the legitimate use of a different lens. As I hope to demonstrate, the resulting understanding of callings involves a greater level of complexity and, hopefully, a more holistic view of an important, often life-changing life experience.

The psychological model of callings that I believe emerges from my interviews with Episcopal aspirants and the writings by those with an interest in the calling process contains a small number of premises, and it is to those that I now turn.

1. Callings can best be understood as strong inner convictions about a certain course of action. They may be experienced as originating outside the person but psychologically are best considered as internal attempts to find meaning by becoming a part of something larger than the self.
2. Callings take time to develop, are difficult to describe, and may go through a series of cognitive phases. Although periods of doubt are common, the predominant affective component of callings is positive.
3. Callings are usefully considered as embedded in the psychological processes of identity formation central to the developmental challenges of adolescence, young adulthood, and middle adulthood.
4. Callings involve a determined effort often involving struggle and sacrifice. Not all those experiencing a call are able to deal successfully with these processes.

5. Callings usually involve support and encouragement from important others. Sharing the call with others may involve fears of rejection.

6. Callings usually appear to arise in a small number of psychological contexts; the healthy-fortunate, the healing marriage, and the crisis-searcher. These contexts underlie what appears on the surface to be considerable variability in the calling experience.

7. Callings appear to be successful efforts to deal psychologically with important developmental challenges and, as such, may be associated with evidence of psychological maturation.

With this emerging psychological model in mind I now turn to the concrete details of my involvement and interview technique. Following that, the focus will be on the findings, then relevant theoretical implications and an overview discussion.

CHAPTER 2

The Process

She was a tall, striking middle-aged woman, both an Episcopal priest and a psychiatrist. Brought to Dallas by a local seminary to teach, her picture began to appear in the newspapers – usually in her long black clerical robe adorned with a large crucifix and marching at the head of various protest parades. At the time I was giving psychotherapy seminars for practicing psychotherapists, and she became a steady attendee. At some point she began calling me to refer friends for individual or couples therapy. We were on a first name, friendly basis but did not see each other socially.

One day she called and asked if I would do her a favor. She went on to explain that her Bishop was about to re-open the temporarily suspended ordination process, a psychiatric-psychologic examination was now mandated as part of the Episcopal ordination process, and she feared that the Bishop would decide in favor of a psychological test format rather than interviews. She knew from my psychotherapy seminars that I had interviewed in depth nonclinical subjects (research volunteers and applicants for a psychiatric residency) and believed that, as a result, I would support her recommendation for an interview format (unheeded, she feared) and help convince the Bishop that interviews were more apt to clarify the psychological status of aspirants than would a sole reliance on paper-and-pencil tests.

I agreed to do so, and we went in 1995 to see the Bishop and the then Canon. I spoke of my experiences with nonclinical subjects and my belief that it was the more effective way to examine aspirants. My priest-psychiatrist friend and I left after a few questions from the two clerics and a week later the Canon called to say they had decided to go with interviews and would like me to be the interviewer.

At a second meeting with the two clerics several issues were clarified. First, I was not an Episcopalian. They responded that such might be an advantage but did not ask about my religious orientation. Second, I suggested that a second examiner, a woman, would be necessary for those aspirants who might prefer such. They agreed. Third was the matter of my fees, and they suggested that my usual psychotherapy fee would be appropriate. I was to bill them and, in turn, they would collect part of the charges from the aspirants.

I next suggested that they have someone in the diocesan office do a literature search on the psychological profiles of successful priests and deacons. They laughed and said that no such studies had ever been done; they doubted that there would be any agreement on defining success in those religious vocations. I then suggested that the purpose of the evaluation appeared to be solely the identification of psychological characteristics that might interfere with adequate functioning as priest or deacon. They agreed, and I responded that predicting effective functioning in any vocation was, at best, a very uncertain business. Severe psychopathology (psychosis and the like) could be reliably identified as well as psychological health. However, there was much middle ground that was hard to assess and might well be relevant for functioning in religious vocations. We remained, therefore, on shaky ground. They acknowledged my assessment of the evaluation process and asked me to go ahead.

In this clarifying interview with the two clerics no mention was made of callings. I learned only later that in the many faceted, lengthy ordination process a candidate's calling was continuously assessed. In the Dallas diocese the assessment process (called "discernment", a softer word) involves a series of meetings with a small committee from the aspirant's parish who then make a recommendation to a larger committee (the Committee on Ministry). After another series of meetings with this committee, the group reports to the Bishop. The Bishop is the final authority and may or may not accept this group's advice. This process of discernment is much the focus of Proctor's book, and she has a great deal to say about the complexities involved in trying to evaluate a person's story of what is experienced as a divine calling.

At this point a review of the psychologic and psychiatric literature did not result in substantial help regarding how to go about the evaluations. I concluded that it was up to me to devise an interview format. The initial interview structure proved useful, and has been changed little throughout the 13 years of its use.

The basic format of the interview was semistructured in the sense that it contained a small number of topics that I introduced and then explored, most often in an open-ended manner much like a psychotherapeutic interview. If the candidate expressed strong feelings, apparent resistances, or other forms of discomfort, I tried to approach the topic with as much tact and sensitivity as possible. "This is really difficult to talk about," "The sadness is right here – still very much alive within you," and "I hear about how difficult the circumstances really were, but in looking back what role do you think you played?" are the sorts of probes that were often used when they seemed indicated.

The usual format was three or four 45-minute interview sessions so each candidate was seen for a total of two to three hours. After a bit of chatting ("Did you have any problems finding my office – it is an out of the way location?"), I asked each candidate if he or she understood what the interviews were about and after listening to their responses, I said, "You know that I write a report to the Bishop, and that you will need to sign an authorization for me to do so?" Only on rare occasions (perhaps several times) did this clarification prompt a response that seemed to warrant exploration.

During the past several years the diocese has changed its processes and now requires both a lengthy autobiographical questionnaire and a shorter mental health questionnaire to be completed by each candidate and in my hands before the evaluation begins. Thus, more recently I refer to the questionnaires, indicating that I have read then, and suggesting (when appropriate) that certain of their responses will need further exploration.

At about this point the first topical area is introduced. The initial topic is almost always the aspirant's experience in his or her family of origin. "Let's start with your early experiences in your family," is a typical opening, and the evaluation begins. Here it may be helpful to the reader if I outline the topics and describe the sought-for information.

1. *Childhood and Family of Origin Experiences*

    After the subject's response to the request to talk about his or her experiences in their families has been explored, specific topics within this domain are introduced (if not reported spontaneously). These include each parent's personality, the nature of the parental marriage, the presence of psychiatric disturbances (depression, alcohol abuse, etc.) the family's economic circumstances, the aspirant's relationship with each parent, experiences of physical abuse, sexual abuse, and gross neglect, sources of affection, and especially close relationships are discussed. Adaptive mechanisms and special roles (the compliant child, the favorite, the rebel, etc.) within the family are explored. Each sibling's life course is obtained. The subject's experiences in school and in friendships are explored. In all of this, apparent contradictions are addressed such as, "You describe a loving family with a great deal of affection and closeness, yet between you and your three sisters there have been 11 divorces. Do you have any thoughts about this?"

2. *Adolescence and Young Adulthood*

    Once again, each subject is asked to describe his or her experiences during these developmental phases. More focused questions are asked to fill in the gaps. In this way the subject's narrative about the earlier years is fleshed out. High school adjustment, academic performance, extracurricular activities, peer relationships, romantic and sexual experiences, drug use, and level of self-esteem are some of the topics introduced. If behaviors suggesting a psychiatric disorder are reported these are explored. College and early work experiences are also discussed. The subject is asked to describe his or her early life dream and the efforts to actuate those hopes and plans.

Early romantic (heterosexual and homosexual) relationships are explored with the goal being to understand the psychological makeup of the chosen partner, the psychological structure of the relationship, its course and outcome.

Work experiences are also explored as they relate to self-sufficiency, self-discipline, attitude towards money, authority, and competition. Significant illnesses and their residual effects are noted, as well as current physical health.

3. Midlife

The aspirants were either facing the challenges of young adulthood (21-39 years), primarily identity, autonomy, and intimacy, or those of midlife (40-65 years) involving re-appraisal of life experiences in work, love, and ideology. In assessing aspirants' midlife adaptation, a series of issues must be kept in the interviewer's mind. These include:

1. Has the subject successfully met the young adult challenges of establishing intimate relationships outside the family of origin and crystallizing a stable sense of identity?
2. Is there evidence that in midlife the subject has been involved in the process of re-appraisal of his or her current life's form and direction in the areas of love and work? Has the process of re-appraisal (including the life dream) resulted in re-affirmation of the status quo or the initiation of attempts to change? Has the re-appraisal process involved solidification or modification of the candidate's system of personal meaning?
3. Is there evidence that the process of transcending purely self-interests has begun? If so, is this process evident in parenting relationships, mentoring, community involvement, and other areas?

4. Marriage and Other Central Relationships

Once again the aspirants are first asked a broad opening question such as "Tell me about the important relationships in your life." Responses are explored as seem indicated. If there have been no significant relationships outside the family of origin, aspirants are asked how they understand that fact. If patterns are reported ("I have an eye for losers"), they are asked how they understand the pattern. When central relationships are noted, questions are asked about the structure of such relationships such as power distribution, level of psychological intimacy, methods of problem-solving, amount and types of physical affection, and overall satisfaction.

When failed relationships are reported, subjects are asked to talk about their roles in the lack of relationship success. "What would your former spouse say about your contribution to the marital failure?" is a type of probe aimed at understanding the capacity for more complex thinking about relationships.

If the subject has children, they are asked to discuss their children, and specific probes are used to get a picture of each child and the relationship with him or her.

Each is also asked about other close, important relationships with siblings, relatives, and friends. In all of this a model begins to be constructed (in my mind) of the subject's balance of separateness and connectedness.

5. *Psychological Characteristics and Self-Image*
"Tell me what it's like to be you", is the usual opening for this section of the interview. It is only after aspirants' responses are explored that more specific questions are asked. They include questions about psychiatric syndromes and, if reported, the nature of any treatment obtained (psychotherapy, psychotropic medications, etc.) and their responses to such interventions. Apart from specific psychiatric syndromes each subject's experience with psychotherapy is explored including why he or she sought psychotherapy, its frequency and duration, and the experienced outcome.

The aspirants are also asked to describe their personalities. After they do so, they are asked to rank themselves regarding a broad array of personality traits (e.g. extraversion-introversion, self-controlled-spontaneous, etc.). They are also asked how much underlying anxiety, sadness, anger, and other affects they must deal with on a more-or-less ongoing basis.

Life crises are discussed, and the coping mechanisms used and their outcomes are also asked about.

In all of this I pay attention to the aspirants' openness or apparent defensiveness. Their ability to think of themselves in terms of complex interactions rather than more simple absolute, either/or terms is also noted. I am interested in ascertaining the nature of the psychological defenses used and their general level of maturity. Finally, in this section two specific questions are asked. One is about recognizing and managing the inevitable internal contradictions, an important developmental challenge of adulthood. The second involves asking what it is that they would like most to change about themselves.

6. *Religious and Spiritual Experiences*

"Tell me about your calling," is the usual opening question for this section. Once again the response is explored in ways that reflect prominent themes and affects. After this general opening, the candidate is asked about childhood, adolescent, and adult religious experiences. The religious orientation of the family of origin is addressed. Intense, time-limited spiritual experiences including conversions, visions, and voices are explored. In regard to the visions and voices the subject is asked whether he or she believed what was seen or heard was actually God (or other religious figures) or originated within the self.

Most of the aspirants did not grow up in the Episcopal Church but turned to it, usually during adulthood. They are asked to describe the factors involved in the change of denominations. Eleven of the aspirants had gone to seminary and been ordained in other Protestant denominations. They, too, were asked to describe the inner and outer circumstances leading to this change.

In obtaining each subject's spiritual and religious narrative, I attempt to locate their experiences within the broader context of what was going on within themselves and at work and in love.

As this brief discussion of the interview format suggests, considerable data are obtained. The other major source of data is their behaviors in the interview situation. How does he or she relate to me? Does the subject seem reasonably comfortable describing deeply personal experiences? Is he or she able to express feelings openly? Is eye contact maintained? How does the subject deal with internal contradictions, randomness, and fate? Does he or she express any interest in who I am and the nature of the report I will write?

7. *The Contributions of The Interviewer*

These questions only begin to tap the complex issues involved in trying to ascertain who the aspirant is from his or her behavior in the interview. In order to make use of such observations the interviewer must have a reasonably clear idea of what he or she brings to the interview format, and what issues the person of the interviewer is likely to evoke. Thus, some personal observations seem necessary.

During the 13 years that I have been doing these evaluations my age has gone from 71 to 84 years. Thus, the first thing that most persons note about me is that I am old. I am also large – well over six feet and still slightly over 200 pounds. I have my hair – now gray – and have dark skin, often tanned from frequent workouts in a swimming pool.

Friends in psychiatry and psychology have told me that I can be an imposing figure – one who speaks well and emanates confidence. My office may add to this image. It is located in a research foundation building and is large and filled with books – some in piles on the floor. The sitting area contains a leather sofa and several comfortable chairs all on an oriental rug. At the end of the room is a large desk filled with reprints and folders and not used in the course of clinical work.

All of this suggests that I am most apt to evoke whatever thoughts and feelings patients (and aspirants) may have about powerful, older men and early transference projections about parental (and, for some, grandparental) figures. This possibility is heightened by my attire – blazers, button-down shirts, subtle ties and, for four or five months a year, seersucker and poplin suits or sport jackets. In short, I suspect that the way I appear suggests an earlier generation and a traditional orientation.

I make a deliberate effort to make aspirants comfortable. In addition to naturally slouching in my chair, I smile frequently and am more empathic than confrontive in exploratory interviews. I may share non-intimate experiences of my own when such seems appropriate.

I also believe that in these two to four evaluation interviews (despite their non-psychotherapeutic nature) there is the opportunity to have a positive (or negative) impact on the candidate's sense of self. As a consequence, I am pleased when a candidate reports that a friend's earlier evaluation was experienced as a helpful, self-clarifying process.

At a different level I bring to the interviews an unusually rich experience with nonclinical subjects. Over the last 50 years I have evaluated the psychological strengths and liabilities of about 800 such persons. Some were volunteers for research projects regarding both functional and dysfunctional families. Others were applicants for a psychiatric residency training program I directed for many years. During more recent years it has been the aspirants for ordination in the Episcopal Church. I have learned that interviewing such persons very often informs one of adult growth experiences not usually heard from those who come for psychotherapy. The latter have had less experience with adult growth experiences, so one hears less about healing marriages, relationships with mentors, teachers, and clergy, spiritual, and other life experiences that initiate, facilitate, or result in adult maturation.

Another consequence of these experiences is my strong interest in longitudinal research projects that systematically follow certain cohorts across much of the lifespan. I believe that I have read most of the books and many of the published papers that have grown out of such studies. I have also participated directly in a longitudinal study focusing on young couples before and after the birth of their first child. All in all, my interest in longitudinal studies and what they teach us about the adult years, has been ongoing since the '60s. Thus, I think I am reasonably well informed on those aspects of the adult self that are most apt to change and those that are relatively stable.

There is more that I bring to the interviews with aspirants. One piece of this is the theoretical lens (really lenses) that I use to interpret what is heard and observed in the interviews. In the context of what is known (longitudinal studies) about adult development, I believe that a small number of theoretical lenses (systems) can be helpful in the attempt to understand a particular person's life. One such system is psychoanalysis with its core premises of anxiety, defenses, internalizations, internal object representations, and the like. Another is attachment theory and the research it has generated. The central idea is that earlier internalizations (internal working models) of relationships with parents and others can be significantly modified by adult attachments including, as I will discuss in a later section, a new relationship with God. I also believe that existential theory as it applies to individual psychological functioning and its particular emphasis on the search for meaning in life can be a very useful way of understanding changes brought about by a variety of adult experiences. In a later section these and other lenses will be discussed as they may apply to callings.

CHAPTER 3

The Findings

At the time of this writing, 108 aspirants have been evaluated. As can be seen in Table 1 the sample is almost equally divided between the genders and on average in early midlife. Women were older than men (avg. 46 years and 40 years respectively) and more likely to be aspirants for the diaconate.

Table 1

Demographic Findings

	N	Male/Female	Avg. Age
Priesthood	76	42/34	41
Diaconate	32	12/20	51
Total	108	54/54	44

Table 2 addresses the developmental stages of the aspirants. As can be noted, all but two of the 42 young adults aspire to the priesthood in contrast to the 66 middle-aged aspirants who are about equally divided between the priesthood and diaconate.

Table 2

Adult Developmental Stage

	N	Male/Female	Priest	Deacon
Young Adulthood (23 – 39 Years)	42	26/16	40	2
Middle Adulthood (40 – 65 Years)	66	25/41	36	30

Current Adaptation

The semistructured, exploratory interview format provided two different approaches to estimating the aspirants' current levels of psychological adjustment. One approach is categorical in that the interview data were considered as discreet variables (e.g., personality traits, level of anxiety, depressive themes, etc.) that could be reliably estimated (and compared to the aspirants' behaviors in the interviews) and then compared to generally accepted guidelines for psychological health and pathology. The second approach to measuring current adaptation relied on the assessment of the life narrative obtained from each subject. In this regard I rely particularly on the thinking and research of McAdams that will be discussed in greater detail in a later section (6). For present purposes, however, what needs emphasis is that certain narrative structures have been found to be correlated with various measures of psychological health. These narrative structures include overall coherence, complexity, tolerance for contradictions and paradoxes, and a balance of the major themes of autonomy and intimacy.

These two ways of dealing with interview data offer a double check on the assessment of level of current adjustment. Despite this precaution, there is a disadvantage to a sole reliance on semistructured exploratory interviews. This involves the identification of mild to moderate personality disorders. Although I believe that both psychological health and the presence of major psychiatric syndromes can be reliably assessed with two to four 45 minute interviews, more subtle forms of personality disorders present a potential problem. They are often – but not always – suggested by frequent job changes, reported problems with anger, impulsiveness, or rigidity, and multiple relationship failures. The question, "What would you most like to change about yourself?" often leads to explorations that suggest mild to moderate personality disorders, as do the aspirants' behaviors in the interviews. In only several of the 108 aspirants, however, were such clues present, and they took the form of defensive avoidance, apparent narcissistic entitlement, and the presence of a struggle with underlying anger. There were also several young men in their early or mid-twenties who had not experienced an emotionally important relationship outside their families of origin and appeared to be unusually dependent on their mothers. Whether these dependencies represent a personality disorder (fixation at an immature level) or, more optimistically, delayed young adult development is an open question.

My concern about the inability of the interview format to identify mild to moderate personality disorders with a high level of confidence is heightened by the belief that such disorders may negatively influence functioning in a religious vocation. This concern is augmented by those priests referred to me for psychotherapy. Although some presented with marital problems, depression, or alcohol dependency, others were referred because of repetitive problems working effectively with a series of congregations and lay leadership. This small group of priest-patients usually presented with mild to moderate personality disorders involving anger and/or psychological unavailability.

With this caveat in mind, what do the interview data reveal regarding current adjustment? First, none of the 108 aspirants appeared to have a discreet current psychiatric syndrome (e.g., depression, alcohol abuse). With but few exceptions these aspirants appeared to be functioning at average or high levels of current psychological health. This healthy functioning was reflected in the categorical approach (e.g., presence or absence of symptoms, pattern of personality traits, etc.), the structure of their life narratives (e.g. complexity, coherence, etc.), and the manner in which they handled the evaluation interviews (openness, warmth, directness, etc.). Only six of the aspirants presented evidence of possible mild to moderate personality disorders. Thus, the strong impression is that, with but few exceptions, this group of young and midlife adults were functioning at reasonable or high levels of psychological health.

This finding is all the more striking when considered in the context of past difficulties. Thirty-four of the 108 subjects presented a clear history of one or more severe adult crises, some of which were described as psychiatric disorders, usually major depression. Twenty-two of the 34 aspirants with histories of adult crises had taken prescribed psychotropic medications (usually antidepressants) and 47 of the total sample of 108 (44 percent) had been or were currently in some form of psychotherapy. Forty of the 108 aspirants (37 percent), mostly young adults, had clear histories of healthy development. Only four of this group described a brief psychotherapeutic experience.

Despite the overall level of average or high psychological health, many of the subjects described the ongoing struggle to change certain aspects of their personalities. Most often this involved the effort to be less self-contained and less structured. "I continue to work on being more spontaneous, more open with my feelings, and more responsive to the feelings of others. I tend to be too analytical – not enough in the moment," one articulate candidate reported. Another said, "I'm still working on trust and intimacy. My history in love relationships is one of being too cautious, reserved, and unavailable."

What is to be made of the clear evidence that most aspirants are functioning at a healthy level? The importance of this question will be emphasized as we turn to their reports of childhood and adolescent experiences in their families of origin.

Families of Origin (FOO)

There are perplexing issues involved in interpreting what people report about their childhoods. One of the foremost is that memory is far from perfect; in fact, there is longitudinal research that demonstrates that what is recalled about childhood is very different during midlife than it was described during adolescence (7). Indeed, many clinicians believe that life narratives are constantly revised, and that the revisions occur outside of the individual's awareness. There are, however, no firm data on who does the most revising of their early experiences or which experiences are most likely to be revised.

A second major issue is that what "really" happens to us early in life – in particular, the nature of our early experiences with caretakers – may have profound effects on subsequent development. This premise, so much a part of clinical thinking, has recently been clearly documented by an exacting longitudinal study of the first 26 years of life (8). This study, along with decades of early attachment research, forms a clear empirical base for earlier theoretical speculations founded on clinical work with adults.

This brief reference to a huge theoretical and research literature is necessary because the childhood experiences reported by this sample of aspirants for ordination in a major Protestant denomination are striking in the number who report clear and often severely dysfunctional families of origin.

The approach used to deal with the data about early family experiences was to classify the reports into one of four broad categories. At the most dysfunctional level, (given a rating of "1"), were reports that included verbal, physical, or sexual abuse or obvious physical and/or emotional neglect. One or both parents were described as significantly flawed, and the parental marriage was conflicted, alienated, or had ended. There was no consistent parental affection or support, and often another relative, minister, or neighbor was reported as the major source of affection and support.

A moderately dysfunctional FOO (classified a "2") involved descriptions of families in which there was little affection and a parental marriage that was unhappy or dissolved. Some such families were rigid, rule-oriented and with little, if any, tolerance for individual differences. A moderately dysfunctional family, however, was not described as abusive or grossly neglectful.

A functional family (rating of "3") was described as one in which one or both parents provided affection and support. The parental marriage was usually intact – although not necessarily happy - and one parent might be clearly more dominant than the other.

An optimal family ("4") was described as open with feelings and both affectionate and supportive of each child's individuality. The parental marriage was recalled as warm, affectionate, and without underlying chronic conflict.

Although this classification system is admittedly a broad-brush approach, it does allow a closer look at these data.

Sixty-four of the subjects reported clearly dysfunctional FOO (29 severely dysfunctional and 35 moderately dysfunctional), and 44 of the subjects reported positive histories of their childhood families (24 functional and 20 optimal). Thus, 61 percent of this sample described a dysfunctional FOO.

The 108 aspirants average FOO score was 2.2. The men generally described their early childhood environments as healthier (avg. 2.6) than did the women (avg. 1.9). Age also appeared relevant. The young adults (39 years or less) FOO average rating was 2.8 compared to the middle-aged average of 1.8. There was no difference in FOO scores for aspirants for the priesthood and those for the diaconate.

Another factor of interest is how the subject recalls responding to the early environment of the family, and whether that response became an important feature of the adult personality. Some response patterns in childhood were described as assigned roles: the parents appear to have decided that one child is the "good" child, for example, and subtly project the message "You must be our good child."

In exploring early family roles (and often their persistence into the adult years) a simple format was used. Four categories were constructed based on the author's previous research and clinical work:

1. The scapegoat or bad child who was oppositional at home and later in school.
2. The parentified caretaker or go-between who either tried to buffer a discordant parental relationship, cared for an obviously disabled parent or sibling, or became the primary source of nurturance and protection for usually younger siblings.
3. The "good" girl or boy, usually very compliant, who attempted to obtain what was lacking in the family (usually described as affection) through accomplishments and behaviors meant to elicit affection or other positive responses.

4. The autonomous role in which the child is encouraged to become his or her own person, to follow personal inclinations, and to explore multiple possibilities for the future.

Among these aspirants 14 clearly described assuming the caretaker, parentified role in childhood. This group described their earlier family environments as dysfunctional (ten as severely dysfunctional), and their average family rating was 1.4. Fifty-seven of the group described themselves as the compliant, "good" girl or boy with most describing a dysfunctional FOO (avg. rating 2.0) and/or memory of having "needed" to be the good child. Thirty-two of the group described themselves as autonomous as children (no recalled pressure to assume any specific role). All but two of these 29 described functional or optimal FOO with an average FOO rating of 3.4.

Thus, in this group of adults, almost two-thirds recalled dysfunctional early family environments and their most common response was to be compliant, to try harder to please. A smaller number – almost all from severely dysfunctional families – described becoming caretakers in early childhood. Not surprisingly, those who described their FOO as encouraging their autonomy also described those families as healthy.

It is difficult to know what to make of these data about childhood and family life. Although they seemed severely skewed toward the pathological, there are no comparable data from representative samples nor from other groups of human services professionals for whom such childhood experiences have been speculated often to be the earliest roots of motivation to enter the helping professions. We shall, however, revisit these data when we search for correlations between the various data modules and look for patterns of psychological factors associated with the calling to a religious vocation.

Midlife Experiences

There is a growing body of data suggesting that adult experiences may alter the effects of early childhood trauma and result in personality growth (9-20). Those experiences most often noted involve caring relationships with a spouse, successful psychotherapy, or positive experiences with a teacher, mentor, priest, minister, or rabbi. Another pathway of adult change involves dealing successfully with life crises, and for some of this sample the resolution of such crises was experienced as basically a spiritual process. For another small group there was no clearly demarcated midlife crisis: rather, a period of several years or more of dissatisfaction and searching for a new direction in life.

This group of aspirants included 76 who are currently married, 16 for the second or third time. Twenty-three of the 108 have never married and eight were divorced and one widowed. Of those currently married, 15 described unhappy or marginal marriages. The other 61 married subjects reported relationships that ranged from "very supportive" to "transforming." Most often the marital relationship was described by this subgroup as a major life turning point. Indeed, 33 of the 61 happily married described either severely dysfunctional (N18) or moderately dysfunctional (N15) FOO, lending weight to the idea of marital healing.

Those subjects who have never married (N23) were either young adults in their 20s (mostly men) or middle-aged women who often presented a history of multiple failed relationships.

Thirty-four described a serious adult life crisis, the resolution of which was seen as a major life turning point. Some of the crises were described as psychiatric disturbances, but for others such a pattern was not present. Most often these aspirants describe the struggle to adapt to the loss of a loved one or a serious career loss. Life crises appeared to be equally distributed between men and women, but, not surprisingly, were much more frequently reported by middle-aged subjects than by younger adults.

The resolution of life crises was most often experienced as a spiritual process, one in which God was centrally involved (and for many a part of the calling to a religious vocation). Some also reported successful psychotherapy as a major pathway and still others described emerging from the crises on their own.

Forty-seven of the group reported a psychotherapeutic experience in the past or currently. For 23 of the 47 the psychotherapy was part of dealing with a crisis. The other 24 aspirants reported that the psychotherapy was the only form of treatment and most often involved attempts to clarify and change dysfunctional relationship patterns. All but one subject described their psychotherapy as helpful, and over half said it was a major turning point in their lives.

Stories of Callings

The responses to the open-ended question, "Tell me about your calling", often began with a disclaimer. "It's difficult to describe." "It's been such a gradual process, and I'm not certain when it began." "I think it began only after my priest talked with me about the diaconate." "I'm not sure how to describe it – the idea of becoming a priest has been inside me off and on for years, but only after my depression did it grow from an idea to more like a conviction, a calling." "I don't know when I didn't feel that doing God's work was who I should be – I can remember thinking that when I was an adolescent." These examples of how some subjects begin their calling stories suggest something of the difficulty that may be inherent in describing spiritual experiences. They also suggest that most persons emphasize the gradual nature of the experience of feeling called. For only a few did the calling begin with a profound, intense spiritual experience, and most of these few described an adolescent or early adulthood conversion experience. Rarely did such a dramatic beginning to the calling story involve the Episcopal denomination. Rather, the early conversion experience more often occurred in a fundamentalist denomination.

The call to ministry for the young adults in the sample was most often described as part of the initial attempt to sort out who one is to be. Whether to be a computer expert, historian, physician, or priest was an internal process that began in adolescence or early adulthood. Often a start was made in one direction and, after several years of effort, increased doubt was experienced, the effort put on hold, and then a new direction established. Levinson's term "searcher" (rather than "tracker") seems particularly suitable for some of these aspirants (21). A small number of young adult aspirants however, did not report this internal searching; rather, their experience of a calling was the only vocation seriously considered ("trackers" in Levinson's view). Most often the decision to pursue the priesthood was congruent with family values and much supported by their parents.

The middle-aged aspirants' callings seemed to clearly reflect the processes of re-appraisal commonly noted during this developmental period. Their careers in business, the professions, and hands-on parenting were, for the most part, clearly successful, but something was missing from their lives. Their callings often grew in the context of some years of investment as volunteers in their parish church. "I've been functioning like a deacon", one candidate said, "and it just seems important to be ordained – kind of legitimizing my work in the church's outreach." For some of these subjects the priesthood was to replace their former occupations, but for others the plan was to gradually cut back on their work as attorneys, for example, and become increasingly focused on their ministry.

The affective quality of feeling called to the ministry was almost always described in very positive terms. Feeling excited, fulfilled, more connected, greater completeness, and other positive descriptors were frequently used. Only a very small number (five) seemed to still be struggling with their sense of being called. Several of these expressed their conflict around the issue of the calling's validity. "At times I wonder if it's really from God?" one such candidate said. Several others of this small group expressed conflict about the overall direction of the Episcopal Church, citing their concern about the election of a homosexual bishop.

A sizeable minority (forty-one of the 108 aspirants) dated the onset of their callings to childhood or adolescent religious experiences. Most often these beginnings were described as embedded in their FOO positive emphases on religious values and practices. For a smaller group a church was described as a caring haven from a severely dysfunctional family.

Finally, the calling narratives often addressed directly or indirectly the search for or a reworking of the person's system of meaning in life. At the most obvious level responding to the calling was expressed as adopting – or, much more often, augmenting – a religious belief system that places one's relationship with God at the center of life's meaning. At a somewhat more inferential level, the theme of self-transcendence seemed obvious. This was particularly noted in the middle-aged aspirants for whom the movement from careers with dominant self-interests to a ministry focusing on the spiritual needs of others was apparent. This theme of self-transcendence appears to mirror what adult developmentalists have described as generativity, and psychoanalytic investigators refer to as altruism, a mature ego defense mechanism.

Thus, this summary of calling narratives emphasizes a small number of characteristics; ineffability, diversity, gradualness, positive affect, support from important others, developmental context, and change in belief about life's meaning. Additionally it seems clear that the subjects experienced their callings as positive changes in their fundamental identity.

There is also the issue of the structure of these stories of callings. If one accepts the observations that spiritual experiences have an ineffable quality and occur over long periods of time, does that mean that these calling narratives lack coherence? Such was not my impression. Despite these problems, most of the aspirants' attempts to describe their callings hung together – they were not incoherent. Further, and especially with the middle-aged aspirants, the calling stories were complex: that is, they involved multiple factors and often an attempt to deal with contradictions. These stories also reflected some of the aspirants' abilities to tolerate uncertainty, to not know and not need to know.

The affective quality of the calling narratives was usually clearly reported but, in addition, some aspirants experienced the affects (and shared them with me) during the process of describing their callings. With these aspirants I felt a greater sense of being drawn into their calling experiences. With those who described their callings without experienced affects, it was more like the two of us were examining the experience at some shared psychological distance.

Thus, despite the real difficulties of finding adequate language to describe the experience of feeling called and the inherent problems of describing what are often very gradual experiences, most of these subjects' stories appeared to reflect a high level of narrative competence.

Stories of Callings Within Life Narratives

In the preceding section the characteristics of calling narratives were described. These narratives, however, are not the whole of each subject's life story. The calling stories are best considered as important ingredients of larger life narratives – narratives, as to be described later – that constitute a basic way that many persons experience who they are. The calling stories are particularly important to the more inclusive life narratives because they describe either the initial direction to which young adults point their lives or as a new direction for the middle-aged aspirants. In the latter instance calling stories can be understood as major life turning points.

If all the interview data are considered, the single finding that leaps out the most is the number of subjects who describe dysfunctional families of origin. Recall that 64 of the 108 interviewees (61%) report adverse early experiences in their families. Twenty-nine of these 64 describe physical abuse, sexual abuse, or gross neglect – hardly minor experiences. The other 35 aspirants describe the absence of affection but not severe abuse or neglect. When these reports of adverse experiences are considered in the context of those longitudinal studies that suggest that adult memories of childhood family experience are more likely to be softened than they are to exaggerate pathology, the reports of these aspirants stand out in even bolder type.

Some sense of the important correlates of these memories of childhood experiences can be seen in Table 3.

Table 3

Family Of Origin (FOO) Correlations

	Functional FOO N44 (39%)	Dysfunctional FOO N64 (61%)
Childhood Roles		
Caretaker	0	14
Compliant	11	45
Autonomous Child	30	2
Crisis-Searcher	8	28
Supportive-Healing	25	32
Marriage		
Psychotherapy	7	40
Psychotropic Medication	2	21

As can be noted, reports of families of origin have clear and unsurprising relationship with other aspects of the subjects' life narratives. Those who describe dysfunctional FOO are much more likely to report childhood roles particularly those of caretaker and compliant, "good" child. Autonomous identities are reported by many more of those describing healthy FOO in contrast to those reporting dysfunctional FOO. Those describing dysfunctional FOO also report more adult life crises and greater usage of both psychotherapy and psychotropic medications. Thus, the descriptions of dysfunctional families of origin are correlated in predictable ways with a variety of adult experiences.

It is also to be noted that many of these aspirants report changes in themselves as a result of their calling experiences. None reported changes that suggest lower levels of psychological functioning. Almost all describe changes in their experienced selves that suggest psychological growth.

The self-reports of change in response to the question, "How has your calling changed you?" involved the subjects' relationships with themselves, with the world, and their elaborating a more detailed, integrated belief system that placed their relationships with God at the center of life's meaning.

The reports of changes in the aspirants' relationships with themselves involved various combinations of the following: reduction or disappearance of symptomatic states such as anxiety or depressive disorders; greater acceptance of self as a flawed, yet lovable person who is in touch with and struggles to integrate his or her internal contradictions; an increased sense of connectedness to others, often described as a greater ability to love; a stronger experience of positive emotions such as peacefulness and contentment coupled with an increased tolerance for uncertainty and doubt.

The reported changes in the subjects' relationships with the world also varied from person to person. Almost all, however, described greater concern for others associated with lessened preoccupation with self-interests. Others reported increased respect for the autonomy of others. "I'm much less inclined to tell people what to do and much more likely to help them sort out their options so they can decide," is the type of statement supporting the increased respect for the autonomy of others.

Another way that some reported changes in their relationships with the world involved the use of the concept of empathy. These subjects described an increased capacity for listening, greater sensitivity to what others are feeling, and better ability to let others know that their feelings are understood.

Although most of the aspirants' religious beliefs and activities were long-standing, their calling experiences appear to have intensified a system of meaning in which one's relationship with God plays a central role. At the same time, it is important to note that relationships with spouses, children, and other family members (as well as close friends) were important and central aspects of the systems of meaning for many.

It is difficult to know what to make of these reported changes growing out of the experience of being called. Responding to the calling sets in motion the long, arduous process of ordination. Many must make significant sacrifices to follow such a course. It is, perhaps, natural to search for and find something good coming out of such a difficult process. From this perspective, the reported changes are in the minds of the subjects. That which argues against this is that many of the changes reported are those that are emphasized by longitudinal researchers as markers of adult growth and maturation. The issue of what to make of self-reports is difficult to resolve and will be discussed in greater detail in a subsequent section.

CHAPTER 4

The Psychological Patterns

Three patterns can be discerned in the subjects' calling stories. Each of the three can be understood as the psychological context of the callings, and an overview of their characteristics can be noted in Table 4. One pattern involves healthy psychological development in mostly young adults with much family support for the choice of a religious vocation (N38). The other two patterns involve difficult beginnings in dysfunctional FOO and the apparent reworking of their residual effects during midlife. One of those two patterns involved callings experienced in the context of a healing marriage (N34). The second pattern was described as callings associated with the resolution of a serious life crisis or the culmination of a long search for identity (N30). Only six of the 108 aspirants did not fit any of the three patterns. These three patterns; fortunate - healthy, healing marriages, and resolution of life crisis-searcher will be discussed below.

Table 4

Psychological Patterns*

	Healthy Fortunate	Healing Marriage	Crisis Searcher
	N38	N34	N30
Dysfunctional FOO	0	34	30
Marital Status			
Positive	26	33	2
Unsatisfactory	0	0	9
Single			
Never Married	12	0	11
Currently Divorced	0	0	8
Widowed	0	1	0
Psychotherapy			
Past or Present	4	19	25
Psychotropic			
Medication	0	5	18

The narratives of six aspirants did not demonstrate any of the three patterns

Fortunate—Healthy Pattern

These subjects reported positive experiences in well-functioning FOO and are predominately young adults, more likely to be male than female and seeking ordination as priests. They describe essentially healthy patterns of adjustment throughout childhood, adolescence, and young adulthood. The major themes of their life stories are good fortune and continuity. They were born into families with a high probability of a good, loving parental marriage. They experienced early and lasting affection from one or, more likely, both parents whose relationship presented a model of adult love. These aspirants were not troubled children or adolescents, although some behind-the-scenes adolescent "acting-out" may have been present involving experimenting with sexuality and/or alcohol. When this occurred, it was often described during the first year or so away from home. Their school adjustment was positive with good grades and involvement in extracurricular activities the rule. Almost all of these mostly young adults aspired to the priesthood.

These aspirants did not report significant episodes of anxiety, depression, or other psychiatric syndromes. Their "difficult times," if they occurred, were usually responsive to losses. Breaking up with a romantic partner, failure to make college grades adequate to get into graduate school, and the accidental death of a good friend are examples of experiences that were difficult and troubling. Only four of the 38 sought help, and this involved talking with a priest and/or a few psychotherapy sessions at a college health service.

Twenty-six of these 38 subjects have a positive, supportive relationship with a spouse. The other 12 aspirants describe earlier committed relationships that did not result in marriage. Most of these are young men and women in their 20s. Several said that their vow of sexual abstinence until marriage was not acceptable to their former partners. Several others reported that their former partners were not totally supportive of their callings, and the relationship ended because of this difference in religious orientations.

This group of aspirants demonstrate a pattern of healthy psychological development beginning with the good fortune of their birth. Most felt parental encouragement to create their own lives without following parental prescriptions. Less than one-fourth felt they had to be the "good child."

For all but a few the experience of a calling was embedded in the strong religious values and practices they were exposed to early in life. Their families were active in their churches, and, although only a few were members of the Episcopal denomination, religion was clearly an important theme of family life. It is, thus, not surprising that these aspirants found family support for their callings. Additionally, some also reported important relationships with priests or youth ministers who encouraged them to consider a religious vocation. The married members of this group also reported strong support for their callings from their spouses as the idea of being married to an Episcopal priest seemed congenial to their own religious value orientations.

There is, however, an obvious contingency to this group's pattern of good fortune, continuity, and psychological health. They are young and have not yet had to face the developmental challenges of midlife with its mandate of re-appraisal, the rigors of the priesthood, and the experience of life's randomness. What can be said, however, is that their developmental experiences up to this point in their lives appear to equip them well to deal with what may be yet to come.

This group of subjects' stories of callings revolve around the developmental challenges of late adolescence and young adulthood. For most of them the calling to a religious vocation was the initial response to the question, "Who am I going to be?" For some, however, the call to ordination was a second or even third answer to that question. Earlier goals involved careers in medicine, law, computer sciences, and the like. Only several expressed any doubt about their calling and for all but these few the calling was experienced as an internal conviction that their path was clear, that becoming a priest was who they were meant to be.

Healing Marriage Pattern

There are now a number of longitudinal studies demonstrating that the nature of a central adult relationship can change the course of life (for better or worse) for persons abused, neglected, or without affection during childhood (9-20). In this sample, 34 report such a healing marriage. This group contains twice as many women as men and is primarily middle-aged.

It is apparent from this group of subjects' life narratives that their early experiences in dysfunctional families – many of which involved severe neglect and/or physical or sexual abuse – had impaired their psychological development. What is striking is that the impairment did not take the form often described as behavior disorders and antisocial personality disorders but of emotional inhibition, compliance, caretaking, and avoidance of closeness. For the more fortunate members of this group a haven was found in a caring relative, teacher, minister, or congregation.

As a group these subjects did well academically but were not often involved in social or extracurricular activities. Many of them left home at the earliest possible time and struck out on their own. This often meant working and paying their own way as part-time college students. They described themselves as capable of friendship but not intimacy. Few of their friends knew about their dysfunctional families. They were, for the most part, constricted emotionally but able to focus effectively on tasks which they performed with high levels of competence.

The underlying scars from their childhoods were reflected mostly in their romantic relationships during late adolescence and young adulthood. Most often they were drawn to flawed partners who needed caretaking but were unable to reciprocate. Some were attracted to abusive men, most often verbally abusive, although physical abuse was sometimes reported. These dysfunctional relationships were often repetitive experiences and sometimes led to marriage and children. Most of this group had to work outside the home, often as the major or only source of family income.

Many in this group turned to religion as an obvious source of solace and support during these years of relationships failures. Caring relationships were often established in their church settings.

The major life turning point, however, was the establishment of a new relationship with a caring partner. For this group these new and different types of relationships led to marriage. The marriages were described as having the characteristics found in our research at Timberlawn Research Foundation exploring the processes involved in healthy or growth-facilitating marriages (22-29). These characteristics included shared power (relatively equal influence on the development of the basic relationship structure), a level of affection satisfactory to both partners (here the reference is to both erotic and nonerotic affection), shared interests and values, and the gradual development of intimate communication (the sharing of vulnerabilities).

In this research each partner tended to ascribe the positive relationship to the other. These subjects were much the same. "He is so reliable, stable, and loving that he's taught me how to be more open, how to really love" is one such example. Another is, "My marriage has turned my whole life around – she is what I've always wanted and needed."

Although we know from longitudinal research that such healing relationships occur, just how they develop remains a mystery. How, after years (often decades) of relationship failures, do some persons find another with whom they co-construct a healing relationship?

It is also important to describe the support and encouragement of the partner for the aspirant's calling. As the interest in a religious vocation intensified, this positive re-enforcement appeared crucial. Most often it occurred in tandem with the encouragement from their rector.

What seems important to emphasize is that these subjects' narratives placed the healing marriage as occurring before the calling and was clearly experienced as an important antecedent of the calling.

This group also frequently reported the positive effects of psychotherapy. Nineteen of the 34 described what they considered to be successful psychotherapy, usually entered into in the effort to understand and change their patterns of relationship failures. Although experienced as very helpful, psychotherapy was not given the centrality accorded to their healing marriages.

Although there is much that we need to learn about this psychological pathway of callings, at the most general level it appears to center on learning how to love; a love that is experienced with a new partner and both changes the residua of harmful early experiences and paves the way for a more intense relationship with a loving God.

Resolution of Crisis—Searcher Pattern

The second group of subjects with narratives of harmful experiences in their childhood FOO describe a very different pathway to a calling. These narratives center about the resolution of a midlife crisis or a long period of searching without a clearly defined crisis. This group of 30 persons is about equally divided as far as gender is concerned and their average age is 46 years.

There are no differences from the healing marriage group in the harmful experiences in their dysfunctional FOO. In both groups there was a near equal distribution of severe dysfunction (abusive and/or neglectful) and moderate dysfunction (lack of affection without abuse or neglect). There was also no difference in the reported response to the family dysfunction.   In this crisis resolution-searcher group the descriptions of responses to their families' flaws – like those of the healing marriage group – emphasized compliance, avoidance, emotional constriction, and caretaking. None of this group responded with open anger or rebellion.

These subjects did well in school but many were relatively uninvolved with their peers. Some found a caring adult in a relative, neighbor, teacher, or minister. As with the healing marriage group, a few found a haven in a church – almost always one they attended without their parents.

The late adolescent and young adult segments of their narratives are much the same as those in the healing marriage group. Most of them left home after high school, and their academic competence enabled them to attend college often while supporting themselves. There is also a similar history of relationship failures with flawed partners. Seventeen had been married with only six describing stable, supportive marriages. These marriages, however, were not described as major turning points in their lives. Rather, their narratives focused on the experience of a severe crisis or period of searching and its resolution.

The crises themselves varied from person to person, although eleven of the group described major depression and four discussed a period of alcohol abuse. The others described turmoil and pain but not clear psychiatric syndromes. Most described a precipitating event, and often these can be understood as losses, a small number involving the actual death of a spouse or other relative. Others described the stress of dealing with a disabled relative, most often a child. Several talked about job or business failures: several more described the crises as involved their leaving abusive spouses or otherwise unsatisfactory marriages.

Twenty-five of the 30 subjects in this group saw a psychotherapist, usually for many months. All but one described the psychotherapeutic experience as helpful, and more than half the group said it was a crucial turning point in their lives. Eighteen of the 30 took prescribed psychotropic medications, which, with rare exceptions, were antidepressants. Most thought the drugs were helpful but a few could not tolerate the side effects.

Although the psychotherapy and medications were described as helpful in the resolution of the crisis, these aspirants placed major emphasis on the spiritual component of their recovery. Although all these aspirants were religious before the experienced crisis, the most common change reported was a new and intensified relationship with God. "I came to feel God's love in a way that is much more intense, much more real than ever before," was said in different ways by many.

Increased and more meaningful prayer was also frequently noted. The helpful support of their priest and/or members of their congregation was also described. Although acknowledging the help they received from psychotherapy and antidepressants, it was the spiritual aspects of their emergence from the crises that was given major emphasis.

The intensified relationship with a loving God led to increased participation in their church's activities and programs, often in leadership roles. Over a period of time – usually several or more years after the crisis – the sense of being called to an ordained role grew. These aspirants explored their early calling with their priests and found encouragement in those relationships.

At the broadest level, if those in the marital healing group first experienced love with a spouse, this group of aspirants described finding love in a new relationship with God. As can be noted in Table 4, however, this new relationship with God has for most not yet led to a new and supportive relationship with a romantic partner.

There is a substantial psychological literature that relates directly to this pattern of change through crises and their resolution. This literature is often called "benefit-finding in adversity" or "post-traumatic growth syndrome" (see, for example, 30-39). Although plagued by the lack of pre-crisis measurements, there is much to suggest that some persons come to function at a more mature level psychologically as the result of their need to deal with adversity. This literature, of course, is related to the long-standing interest of theologians and philosophers in the purpose of suffering. What seems particularly pertinent to the purposes of this report, however, is that those psychologists who have addressed the changes resulting from coping with adversity have often placed major emphasis on the subjects' struggle to both find meaning in the adversity and, often, to modify their basic systems of meaning. These scholars often report that systems of meaning that are basically religious are often intensified by the struggle with adversity. This, of course, is precisely what is reported by this group of aspirants. Their callings to ministry can be understood as growing out the intensified religious belief system, itself a result of the struggle to resolve a severe life crisis.

Before turning to other findings of the study, brief descriptions of several other groupings of subjects may be helpful. First, only six of the 108 aspirants did not fit into one of the three groups. Although each of these described dysfunctional FOO, none of them described either healing marriages or a crisis resolved by a new relationship with God.

Twenty of the 108 aspirants (19%) reported an intense, time-limited spiritual experience lasting several minutes to a day or so. The experiences occurred during adolescence or the adult years and were recalled vividly. Eight described their spiritual experiences as occurring during a period of stress or crisis. Several others reported such experiences during church or revival services. Ten of the 20 described an intense experience of God's presence: several heard God's voice. They felt strong emotions – most often described as peace, awe, and a strong sense of connectedness or oneness. Several aspirants reported that the intense, spiritual experiences directly involved the feeling of being called to the ministry; for others the experiences both reflected and were part of their strong religiousness but were not described as part of their calling.

These 20 aspirants are those who describe what sounds like adult experiences of self-transcendence. They do not, however, differ from those without such experiences as far as age, gender, FOO dysfunction, life crises, quality of marriage, or other variables.

Mention should also be made of those 11 aspirants who were ordained originally in another Protestant denomination. These 11 were all men and, with the exception of one, were seeking ordination as priests. Their ages ranged from 34 to 58 years with an average of 44 years (exactly those of the entire group of 108). Four were ordained in the Baptist Church, two in the Methodist Church, and the other five each represented a single other denomination.

These 11 men most frequently described their motivation as revolving around their attraction to the sacraments and liturgy of the Episcopal Church. Their callings to the earlier ministry almost always occurred in late adolescence or young adulthood and each had spent about 20 years in that ministry. Some reported a midlife crisis; others a new and healing love relationship. Some of them described a friendly relationship with an Episcopal priest which facilitated their interest in changing denominations.

It should also be noted that for many of the other aspirants the change in vocation is even more dramatic. Of those seeking ordination as priests several came from business careers – usually of a managerial type. Four had been masters-level psychotherapists, three were leaving their careers as attorneys, two had careers as nurses, one as a pharmacist, and perhaps surprisingly one was leaving his successful career as a police detective.

Another large group (N22) had been centrally involved in careers as wives and mothers. Their callings represented a major change in their core identities.

Thus, it seems realistic to understand the change in direction of the 11 subjects with prior ordination in another denomination against the backdrop that the callings that come in midlife to all aspirants reflect change; change in life's direction, change in life's priorities, and change in narrative identity.

Evidence For Psychological Growth

I have discussed this subject in earlier sections, but wish to emphasize it more fully at this time. First, however, a note to those not familiar with the literature regarding adult development and change. Longitudinal studies have demonstrated clearly that important aspects of personality continue to change during the adult years. Although personality traits (e.g. extraversion, conscientiousness, etc.) are least likely to change other personality characteristics (e.g. relationship competence, defense mechanisms, etc.) often change during the adult years. Further, the most frequently noted mechanisms of adult change involves the internalization of those we love and love us in return. Adult personality changes, it is thought, through the medium of relationships. Healing marriages and relationships with psychotherapists, ministers, close friends, mentors, and others are most often noted. There is also – as mentioned earlier – a great deal of data about growth through dealing with adversity.

The qualitative interview data from these subjects contain two sets of data suggesting that calling experiences are associated for some with adult psychological growth. The first involves the nature of the self-reported changes. I have earlier in this text suggested that the changes can best be described in three categories: changes in the experience of the self; changes in relationships with the world; and changes in the expressed system of personal meaning. I will not repeat here all the particulars of these changes; rather a summary would highlight a greater acceptance of one's self with moderation or disappearance of earlier psychological symptoms and increased tolerance of uncertainty, doubt, and internal contradictions. The self-reports of changed relationships involved greater emphasis on the importance of relationships, increased empathy, and a new emphasis on altruism. The changes in belief systems centered about a stronger sense of connection with God and increased emphasis on close relationships with others.

These three interrelated categories of self-reported changes bear a strong likeness to the nature of adult developmental growth as illuminated by longitudinal observations of diverse samples. They are important dimensions of adult psychological health. It is unlikely that the aspirants had any direct awareness of the findings of these longitudinal studies, and I take these self-descriptions as suggestive of adult psychological health.

The second set of interview data suggesting positive changes involves the clear description by almost two-thirds of this sample of often severely abusive and neglectful early childhood experiences, and my observations of their behavior in the evaluation interviews with me. They clearly appeared to be functioning (with only a few exceptions) at average or high levels of psychological health. In addition, their autobiographical narratives were (again with few exceptions) of the type described as most characteristic of persons with higher levels of psychological health. That is they demonstrated complexity, coherence, and acceptance of contradictions.

These two sets of related data suggest the development of more mature levels of psychological health, often after some years of psychological struggle. The relationship of the calling experience, however, to the suggested adult maturation is not clear. Although I will discuss this issue more completely in a later section, here the central issue will only be mentioned. What is the relationship between the experience of being called and psychological growth? Does the calling lead to growth, reflect that growth, or are the two experiences (calling and growth) related to each other in a circular manner? Clearly the issue is complex.

CHAPTER 5

Discussion

The two findings from this qualitative study of callings are that, with few exceptions, the 108 aspirants for ordination in the Episcopal Church described one of three psychological pathways to their callings, and those callings appear to be associated with descriptions of personality maturation. Not surprisingly, preliminary studies such as this one raise more questions than they answer. Actually, that is their purpose. They are meant to provide hypotheses to guide more focused studies.

The finding of three psychological pathways to the calling experience illustrates this point. The three pathways are not all that remarkable. There are many fortunate persons born into healthy families with strong religious values and only a few of these ever experience a calling to a religious vocation. What else is involved in those 38 subjects who reported this pattern? That there is something else involved speaks to the complexity of all human behavior – that there are inevitably multiple factors that play causative roles. A psychological understanding of callings will involve several, probably many causative influences.

In this time of rapid advances in the neurosciences it is increasingly apparent that all personality traits have a genetic component. This is not to be thought of as a fixed one-to-one relationship between gene and behavior, rather that almost always multiple genes produce a propensity to a certain trait that is then facilitated (or not) by experiences. Is there a possibility that one of the factors influencing the callings of these 38 subjects is genetic? Of course there is such a possibility, and I will discuss that shortly.

One would also want to examine more closely than possible in this study the possibility that certain childhood and/or adolescent experiences will help us better understand why these 38 subjects in the healthy-fortunate group experienced a calling. Here the possibilities are numerous. Could it be the dynamics of a particular early relationship with a parent? A certain type of attachment experience with mother and/or an early identification during adolescence with a minister or deeply religious and emotionally important adult are but two examples. In focusing on relationship experiences the emphasis is placed on the dominant theory of psychological maturation across the life span: the taking into the self those persons or their characteristics who we love and love us in return. This taking in process (internalization) will be described in greater detail shortly.

The other two groups – the healing marriage and crisis-searcher aspirants present similar issues. Only a few of those experiencing either a healing marriage or resolution of a crisis experience a call. These adult experiences are noted as pathways of overcoming the enduring residual effects of early life trauma and, as such, lead to personality maturation in many. Few, however, experience a calling to a religious vocation. What distinguishes the few who do from the many who do not? Again the possibilities are many. Are there particular types of relationships that increase the probability of such experiences leading to a call? Are there particular types of pre-existing belief systems that are involved? Recall that almost all of these 70 subjects were religious before their healing marriages or crises. Could it be as straightforward as believing in a certain kind of God? A recent study, for example, identified four different images of God in a large representative sample (40). These four were the Authoritarian, the Benevolent, the Critical, and the Distant. Could it be that callings are more likely if the person's concept of God is Benevolent (loving and involved directly in one's life) than if it is Distant (uninvolved in persons' lives, more a cosmic force in nature)?

There is also the possibility that one of the factors involved in callings has to do with the brain. The remarkable advances in neuroscience have resulted in the finding that the brain continues to change during the adult years and that changes are prompted by certain experiences. There is interest in the impact of prayer and meditation on brain growth, and the idea that callings might be influenced by the strength of certain brain circuits (and, in turn, alter those circuits) is no longer considered preposterous.

I will explore these matters in more detail in what is to come. To do so involves dipping into a small number of theories of psychological functioning for relevant constructs. This "pick and choose" approach is necessitated, as pointed out by Weagraff, because there is not a systematic, developmental psychology of callings (41). Before turning to the theories of psychological functioning, however, the work of the late Jerome Frank needs to be described (42, 43). Frank was one of my generation's most astute students of psychotherapy. His approach was to look at all the different types of psychotherapy and search for what they had in common. Thus, Frank's work goes beyond any particular theory of psychological functioning. What is of particular importance for present purposes is that he included other experiences known to change individuals' basic belief systems, or what he called their assumptive worlds. Frank thus reviewed carefully what is known (scientifically) about such diverse experiences as religious conversion, revival experiences, and religious healing as well as thought reform (persuasion) and the placebo effect (expectations).

Frank concluded that changes in persons' psychological functioning came about when their systems of meaning were altered. Four major commonalities were found:

1. An emotionally charged relationship with a helping person (often with the participation of a group).
2. A healing setting that provides both safety and hope.
3. A rationale, conceptual scheme, or myth that provides a plausible explanation for the person's dilemma and prescribes a ritual or procedure for resolving it.
4. A ritual or procedure that require the active participation of the person and one or more others who believe that the procedure will be efficacious.

It does not take much imagination to suggest that Frank's four commonalities may apply to the maturation associated with callings. Callings involve an emotionally charged relationship with God and are supported by important others. The healing setting may be experienced by many as the congregation. The rationale involves the shared belief that there are persons who are called to God's ministry. This rationale leads then to the ordination process. So, it seems a case can be made that Frank's four commonalities can apply to the calling experience and the resulting changes in the called person's self-system. Although Frank does not specifically discuss callings (there has been no scientific work), he does write:

". . .it is hard to conceive of a greater source of inner strength and personal security than the conviction that one is God's chosen instrument" (42, p. 81).

And this from a secular psychiatrist who spent his professional life studying effective psychotherapies!

I will now turn to a further explication of a small number of psychological constructs from different theories that are useful in thinking about the calling experience.

One way to think about these theories is that they emphasize different perspectives on personality maturation. Gene-environment interactions, although perhaps not yet a formal theory, is a rapidly emerging paradigm of human behavior and is included because of the intellectual excitement associated with it. Health and psychopathology are believed to result from the ways that genes and experiences interact.

The dominant premise regarding personality maturation continues to be the taking-in (internalization) of those we love whose internal representations become a central part of one's self. Both psychoanalytic theory and attachment theory emphasize this taking-in process and will be briefly described.

Another approach to how persons change is essentially cognitive. Personality maturation occurs when persons' beliefs about themselves and the world change. Existential theory emphasizes that growth occurs through the process of changes in the individual's system of meaning. Narrative theory also addresses change through cognitive processes, although here the change occurs in the person's life narrative or, perhaps more specifically in the process of narrating a new autobiographical self. I will also address these two basically cognitive theories in what follows.

Gene—Environment Interactions

I begin with this theoretical lens because it seems to be an emerging paradigm for understanding all behavior. Its major premise is that genes effect the environment, (e.g. the extravert produces a different response than the introvert), and in turn, the environment (e.g., stress) may turn on and off the activity of genes. Thus, genes and environment have a circular relationship with each other.

This paradigm's rapid development springs from several sources. First, quantitative behavioral genetics (twin and adoption studies) has demonstrated that most, if not all, aspects of personality have a genetic component. Thus, persons are born with varying propensities for different behavioral traits, and these propensities are, to one extent or another, then shaped by developmental experiences. The second source of the gene – environment interaction lens are the findings from recent longitudinal studies (44, 45). These demonstrate that several psychiatric disorders result both from abnormalities in certain genes involved in the brain's neurotransmitter systems and certain life experiences. Both the genetic factors and the environmental factors are required: neither by themselves is sufficient to produce the disorder. As exciting as these studies are, there are no similar studies of gene-environment interaction in normal development or psychological health.

This paradigm has not to my knowledge been applied to spiritual experiences in general or to callings in particular. It does, however, direct attention to several basic questions. First, are there data suggesting that genetic factors influence religious values and activities? Are some persons born with the genetic predisposition to be religious, to be drawn to a certain denomination, or to be called to God's ministry? These questions – hardly imaginable but a few decades ago – can now be seriously raised.

The second basic question prompted by this theoretical lens involves environmental factors. What types of life experiences can be understood to activate (or deactivate) the underlying genetic predispositions to various religious attitudes and activities – including callings?

There are data from twin studies suggesting that certain religious values and activities may have an inherited component. The study that has attracted the most attention is the Minnesota Study of Twins Reared Apart (MISTRA) (46). In this research 53 pairs of monozygotic twins reared apart (MZA) and 31 pairs of dizygotic twins reared apart (DZA) were compared along a wide range of personality variables including several religious characteristics. Data from another 1642 twins' responses were also used. The MZA showed a greater concordance than the DZA on religious fundamentalism, religious interests, and interest in religious occupations. The investigators concluded that roughly 50 percent of the differences between MZA and DZA were due to genetic influences. Thus, this study demonstrates a possible hereditary component to religious callings.

MISTRA has been well-publicized in the lay press and has had clear impact on the way mental health professionals think about the genetic influence on personality characteristics. A resounding critique of MISTRA's methodology has, however, not attracted such attention. Joseph described the ways in which the research methodology was seriously flawed and, in particular the refusal of the investigators to share raw data (rather than only group averages) with other scientists (47). Joseph's analysis raises – at least for this reader – serious questions about MISTRA's conclusions.

Fortunately, there is another twin study with better methodologies that includes several religious variables. Unfortunately, however, interest in religious vocations was not one of the studied variables. The "Virginia 30,000" study reports on a population–based sample of over 14,000 twins and their family members (48). Although the strongest predictor of religious variables involves family influences, religious conservatism and church attendance showed moderate correlations among twins. These were stronger for monozygotic twins than they were for dizygotics. Thus, some religious variables appear to have a genetic influence. The idea that callings may have a genetic predisposition remains unproven, but the twin studies allow us to retain that possibility.

There is another approach to exploring this question. This involves the construct of self-transcendence. There appears to be widespread agreement that self-transcendence refers to the experience of oneself as part of a larger whole and a sense of oneness. It is usually God or nature that the person feels at one with, but it can be human groups, causes, or ideals that come to be central to one's experienced identity. The affect associated with experiences of self-transcendence is almost always very positive and is most often described as deeply peaceful.

The slipperiness of the construct involves whether to consider self-transcendence as primarily a brief period of altered consciousness or a more or less constant personality trait. If it is considered a specific alteration in consciousness that presumably all persons might experience, it is of limited value in thinking about callings. (Recall also that less than 20 percent of the aspirants report such intense experiences and only some of these relate them to their callings). If, however, self-transcendence is considered primarily a personality trait that individuals manifest to a greater or lesser extent, then it becomes plausible to consider that persons with greater propensity for such experiences might be more likely to experience callings. That is, of course, yet to be demonstrated.

d-Aquili and Newberg have studied brain activity during periods of peak self-transcendence in meditation and prayer (49). They found similar changes in these two groups in brain areas believed to be involved in the delineation of the physical self in space. They suggest that experiences of oneness involve complex circuits that are particularly reflected in special brain areas. More to the point regarding the personality trait approach to understanding such experiences, they also suggest a continuum of oneness. Beginning with "baseline reality" the continuum moves to aesthetic experiences (sunsets and symphonies) to romantic love and then to certain spiritual experiences and on to "cosmic consciousness" and trance experiences. Presumably most person's personalities equip them to experience aesthetic and romantic love types of consciousness with fewer able to experience spiritual oneness and even fewer the cosmic and trance levels of consciousness.

The most direct approach to self-transcendence as a personality trait is the work of Cloninger (50). He included self-transcendence as one of seven scales in a self-report personality inventory. This measure of self-transcendence has a genetic component (twin studies) and is positively correlated with the frequent use of meditation and prayer. Two other efforts to relate Cloninger's self-transcendence scale to specific genes involved in neurotransmitter metabolism identified two different genes that were, however, very weakly correlated with that scale (51, 52).

Thus, although there are no data regarding a possible biology of callings, there is, in sum, enough research to suggest that there may be genetic factors involved in some spiritual experiences and activities. As a consequence, the possibility that callings may have a biological component needs not to be dismissed.

When it comes to the types of life experiences that may turn on or off whatever genetic predispositions exist, the callings of the subjects reported here suggest certain types of positive relationships (supportive, loving families, healing marriages), and an intensified relationship with God growing out of the struggle to overcome adversities.

Thus, the emerging paradigm of gene-environment interactions offers a previously unthought of way of looking at callings. Whether it will actually prove to be useful awaits research efforts which, to my knowledge, are not yet even on the drawing board.

Psychoanalytic Theory

If a closer relationship with God is a part of the process of religious callings, there are several key psychoanalytic constructs that need to be briefly discussed. One way to understand a closer relationship with God is as an internal experience that is defined as taking into oneself a stronger sense of God whose work one is called to do. Psychoanalytic theory emphasizes the process of "taking into the self" in its emphasis on internalizations and internal self and object representations.

There is a huge literature on these topics, and I will only briefly outline my understanding of these complex processes. After doing so a recent report from a longitudinal study supporting these processes will be noted, and then, an example of one theologian's use of them as a framework for understanding a person's relationship with God will be reviewed.

Although internalization is a key construct in psychoanalytic thinking, we know very little about those processes that underlie it, and internalizations remain in some ways a mystery. Vaillant, a psychoanalytic longitudinal investigator, has attempted to clarify this construct (53). It should be emphasized that his longitudinal data support the premise that maturation of the ego (equate with personality growth) occurs throughout the lifespan and the central mechanism of this maturation is the internalization of those we love. Using clinical examples, Vaillant describes a hierarchy of internalizations that ranges from those that do not result in personality growth (e.g., incorporation, introjection) to those that do (e.g., idealization, identification). The former are characteristic of immature personality structures and the latter of those that are more mature. He uses also the metaphor of "metabolism" – internalizations have to be somehow "digested" by the self in order to become a part of the self. Vaillant acknowledges that we know very little or nothing about these digestive processes, and his use of such a metaphor speaks to that fact.

The brief discussions of internalization lead us to the central premise of the now-dominant psychoanalytic perspective, object-relations theory (54). The premise is that from infancy throughout the lifespan important persons are taken into the self and become the central psychological structures of the self. Object-relations theory states that the resulting internal representations are of two types, self and other, and involve two different affective components, good and bad. Under the best of circumstances the developing infant's self comes to be comprised, in the main, of internal representations of a good self and a good object. At the opposite extreme the infant's self is comprised mostly of bad self and object representations. These representations grow out of early experiences with primary caretakers and form the core structures of the developing self. Cognitive theory and attachment theory share closely related ideas of personality development.

More than anyone else Kohut, the founder of self-psychology, extended these ideas into the adult years (55). He emphasized that we never entirely lose our need for self-validating others who we internalize in order to modify earlier distortions of the self resulting from negative infant and childhood representations.

As can be readily understood, internalizations and the resulting self and object internal representations are remarkably difficult to study in systematic ways. A recent and remarkable developmental study, however, presents a start – at least as far as measuring internal self and object representations is concerned. Sroufe and his colleagues summarize their remarkable study of 180 disadvantaged persons starting during their prenatal periods and extending into young adulthood (8).

Space does not permit me to describe fully this wonderful study. For purposes of this book, however, the investigators' approaches to measuring internal self and object representations and the ability of such to predict the outcome of the next developmental phase and, in turn, to be altered by the developmental experiences of that phase is the most systematic approach to these important constructs of which I am aware. The investigators used rigorous research methodologies in objectifying internal representations and, for present purposes, were able to not only document their nature but also demonstrate both their predictive and responsive nature. Thus, their measures of infant representations predicted preschool behaviors which, in turn, predicted continuity or change in school-aged representations and so on into early adulthood. Although their guiding theory was not explicitly psychoanalytic, their findings provide support for the psychoanalytic constructs of internalizations and internal self and object representations.

The reader may well wonder what all this has to do with God, religion, and callings? The answer is that a few psychoanalysts and theologians have suggested that psychoanalytic object relations theory is a useful lens through which to better understand religious experience. Rizzuto is one of the few psychoanalysts who has written about God as an internal object representation (56). She uses psychodynamic interview data (18 hours), a questionnaire, and a projective, "draw a picture of God" technique from a sample of 20 psychiatric patients. The major thrust of her writing is the articulation of a theory of God from an object relations perspective. Her theory begins with the premise that a person's concept of God is a result of conscious thinking, the agenda of theologians and other thinkers and needs clear demarcification from a person's internal God representation. The latter, she writes, is present in all persons and arises in childhood, primarily from internalized parental representations. Although the God representation is influenced by subsequent experiences, it is within each person across the lifespan. Nonbelievers are those who have decided (for conscious or unconscious reasons) not to believe in a God whose God representation is within. The God representation has its own developmental trajectory and often plays a crucial role in the development of the self.

Howe, a Protestant theologian, writes that, in addition to the reality of God's existence, it can be useful to consider God as an internal object representation (57). In his view the internal representation of God is the product of a wide array of memories, is impacted by parental and other internal representations, and, in turn influences the quality of those representations. Thus, for Howe, the internal representation of God may play an important role in the development of the self.

Howe also suggests that it is useful to consider a person's internal representation of God as a transitional object, that is a soothing presence (much like the early good parent) needed across the life cycle at times of transition when the safe familiar must give away to a new uncertainty.

Although there are others who write about the usefulness of using psychoanalytic object relations theory in understanding the role of God in the lives of some persons, it is, perhaps, more to the point to ask what the implications are of such a view for the topic of callings to religions vocations.

There are no systematic data informing us regarding God as an internal object representation and any spiritual experiences including callings. As indicated above, it has only been recently that Sroufe and his colleagues devised measures to discriminate internal object representations and their role in development (8). That study did not include God, spiritual experiences, or callings. Thus, what we are left with are theoretical premises. If God can be reasonably considered as an internal object representation, and if a calling to a religious vocation can be considered a new or reworked relationship with God then the use of an object relations perspective in our understanding results in a coherent premise. It is to be recalled that from a psychoanalytic perspective the major pathway of psychological growth involves the internalization of those we love and who love us in return. This premise can readily be applied to a person's relationship with God, the resulting internalization and new or strengthened internal object representation would be considered a pathway of personality growth for some persons.

Attachment Theory

The next theoretical lens through which to view the psychology of callings, attachment theory, is of particular importance because it has generated a body of research regarding God as the ultimate secure attachment figure. This research does not directly explore the calling experience but clearly has significant implications for a beginning understanding of its psychology. First, however, a brief introduction to attachment theory.

Bowlby, a psychoanalyst, formulated attachment theory, and Ainsworth developed a method of identifying an infant's security of attachment to the caretaking adult (58-61). Her method, The Strange Situation, involved exposing the usually year-old infant to a series of brief separations and reunions from and with the caretakers. A small number of distinct types of reactions were clearly noted. Most infants (50-60%) were securely attached in that they protested the separation and were soothed by the reunion. Another group (20-30%), described as avoidant attachment, neither protested the separation nor responded to the reunion. A third group (anxious-ambivalent) comprised 15-20% of most samples protested the separation but were clingy and not soothed by the reunion. The Strange Situation method led to thousands of early developmental studies demonstrating that infantile attachment type has predictive value for subsequent childhood and adolescent development. These studies have been understood to basically confirm Bowlby's contention that early attachment experiences lead to an internal working model of relationships that serves (unless modified) as a template for subsequent relationships. Here, again, the taking-in process is emphasized.

Attachment researchers soon turned to adult relationships and developed several approaches to measuring adult attachment type (secure, avoidant, and anxious-ambivalent) (62, 63). Securely attached adults are comfortable with both emotional closeness and independent activities. Adults with avoidant attachment styles are of two types, dismissive and fearful. Both types avoid closeness and dependency and appear very independent. Those with anxious-ambivalent adult attachment styles are anxious about their ability to develop close relationships and uncomfortable without them.

Several longitudinal studies have demonstrated considerable stability for adult attachment types with, for example, 83 percent of secures showing stability across a four year period in contrast to 61 percent of avoidants and 50 percent of anxious-ambivalents (64).

Adult attachment behaviors are activated under stress, particularly the threat of or actual loss of an important other person. Many systematic studies have explored the relationship between loss (and other stressful situations) and attachment behaviors. These studies will not be reviewed here for reasons of space. The overall conclusions of these studies emphasizes that securely attached adults (in contrast to avoidant and anxious-ambivalent) are more apt to feel less threatened in stressful situations and more readily turn to important others for support.

Before turning to the research exploring attachment types and religious variables, a few comments seem necessary about the characteristics of persons who are most psychologically available for secure attachment relationships. First, they show secure attachment styles of their own. Second, they are emotionally available, sensitive to the feelings of others, and capable of supportive, soothing behaviors with important others. These characteristics are of particular importance because those investigators who have explored the relationships between attachment types and religious variables often conceptualize God as the ultimate secure attachment object – the "other" who understands and supports one in times of stress.

I cannot review all of the studies in this area; rather, the focus will be on some of the work of Kirkpatrick and his colleagues who have been leaders in this field (64-68).

First, there appears to be a correspondence between secure adult attachment type and stronger religious beliefs and greater religious activities. A different picture emerges, however, when examining early childhood attachment types and adult religious beliefs and activities. Those persons with insecure (avoidant and anxious-ambivalent) childhood attachments (with their mothers) report much higher rates of change in religious beliefs and practices during adolescence and adulthood. That is, they are much more likely to experience religious conversions and other spiritual experiences. Thus, Kirkpatrick suggests that for some persons with insecure childhood attachments God may serve as a secure attachment figure, a haven of safety and support. Indeed, entering such a new relationship with a loving God can be understood as a growth experience. In this way Kirkpatrick echoes the early observations of William James who described conversion psychologically as growth from fragmentation to integration (1).

Although there is no mention of callings in Kirkpatrick's writings, his research raises the unexplored issue of the relationship of callings to conversion experiences. Can, for example, callings be usefully considered a subtype of conversion? Is, as I have suggested earlier, it useful to consider conversions as a newfound belief system ("This is what I believe") and calling as a newfound identity ("This is who I am")? There is, however, no consensus on this distinction.

Kirkpatrick does suggest, however, several possibilities that relate to two of the three psychological pathways to being called. He describes how those with insecure childhood attachments (comparable, without too much of a stretch, with the aspirants' descriptions of dysfunctional childhood family environments) may enter a new love relationship which results in a secure attachment. This newfound secure attachment can then lead to a new secure attachment with God. This, of course, is precisely what those aspirants with healing marriages described as the context of their being called to God's service.

Kirkpatrick's other pathway emphasizes how a new and secure attachment to God may then lead to a new and secure relationship with a love partner. This sounds much like the descriptions of those aspirants who described serious midlife crises with a resolution strongly influenced by spiritual factors as the context of their callings. At the time of my evaluations of these aspirants, however, only a few reported new and secure love relationships. Perhaps for some such experiences are yet to come.

I am hopeful that this very brief summary of attachment theory and research conveys something of the appeal of this theoretical lens. More than any other theoretical approach attachment theory has led to systematic research, and its extension into the interface of religion and psychology has resulted in some very promising leads to a better understanding of the psychology of callings.

Existential Theory

One does not have to go very far into the literature on the relationship between adult change and existential constructs to be impressed by several observations. First, existential theory is not tightly constructed; rather it has a heavy stream of amorphousness. Many years ago Havens, in his wise dissection of the four schools of psychiatry (objective-descriptive, psychoanalytic, interpersonal or social, and existential) wrote that existential theory had been little embraced by American psychiatry, partly because of its diffuseness (69).

The second observation is the pervasiveness of the belief that adult change inevitably involves changes in the individual's system of meaning. In fact, some students equate personality change with change in belief systems: it is not that the two are associated rather they are the same thing. This observation – essentially about the nature of change – is found most frequently in the literature on growth through adversity (the post-traumatic growth syndrome). This literature, however, is mostly concerned with subjects' stories of adversity, personality growth, and changed systems of meaning without observational data from both pre- and post-traumatic periods. Exactly what to make of the perplexing issue of historical versus narrative validity will be discussed in the section on narrative theory.

A third observation from this literature is the strong intuitive appeal of the existential perspective regarding personality change in general and that associated more specifically with the experiences of being called to God's service. How can callings not be understood as reflecting either an intensification of a previously held religious system of meaning or the development of a new religious system of meaning? This issue will be explored at the end of this section: Here I wish but to note the strong intuitive appeal of the association of callings and systems of meaning.

These personal impressions of the literature serve as an introduction to a brief description of those aspects of existential theory as I believe they may apply to callings. At the center of this theory is the premise that there is a small group of concerns or anxieties that is universal; that is present in the unconscious of all persons. Further, these "ultimate concerns" are at the very core of the personality. Yalom's descriptions of four ultimate concerns has been most useful (70). He describes the four as meaning, death, freedom, and isolation. To be human involves the fundamental need to find or construct the meaning of one's life. This may involve the conscious elaboration of a meaning system or in its absence a set of behaviors from which underlying values can be inferred (71). Using his holocaust experiences Frankl has been an outstanding proponent of the central importance of the search for meaning in understanding personality (72).

Death and anxiety about it is another of the four ultimate concerns. Here the focus is primarily upon deeply unconscious fears of death that are so frightening as to be rigorously excluded from consciousness. Ernest Becker is the writer who has explored this ultimate concern in greatest detail (73). He suggests that it is the dominant ultimate concern for most people and the psychological defenses erected to keep it from consciousness are a major force in shaping the entire personality.

Both the fears of meaninglessness and death are often noted in discussions of adult development and maturational changes. The other two ultimate concerns have prompted much less attention. Freedom or groundlessness, as it is often referred to, involves the realization that life's outcome is the result of one's decision-making: try as hard as possible to deny it, circumstances play but a minor role. This ultimate concern may have attracted less attention because it is such a radical individualism, avoiding the demonstrated impact of a wide array of educational, socio-economic and other social forces.

The fourth ultimate concern, isolation, is described as different from isolation from parts of the self or important others. It is a profound fear that, despite important connections to others, one is, in the end, alone in the universe. This ultimate concern, like freedom, has attracted much less theoretical and research attention than the fears of death and meaninglessness in those interested in adult change.

Yalom's discussion of the interrelatedness of the four ultimate concerns emphasizes that these basic personality variables rarely act independently (70). More recently Baumeister has written a detailed account of the psychology of meanings (4). His emphasis is on identifying why establishing a sense of meaning in one's life is so important. He suggests that four needs are involved; purpose, value, efficacy, and self-worth. A person's need for meaning is the product of his or her need to believe that life has a purpose or goal, that his or her behavior in pursuit of that goal or goals is right, good, and justifiable. Further, the individual needs to feel that he or she is strong and competent in pursuit of life's goals and, as a consequence, can feel good about himself or herself. Baumeister, goes on to note that persons' searches for meaning tend to focus on religion, relationships, work, and selfhood.

Emmons is another contemporary student of meanings (74). He suggests that spirituality can be defined as the search for meaning, for unity, for connectedness. The most important function of spirituality is providing a unifying philosophy of life that confers coherence upon the personality. Thus spirituality – and, more generally, religion – can lead to transformation of the personality – from fragmentation to integration, from separation to reconciliation. Emmons reviews the research literature exploring the impact of the search for meaning on personality functioning and concludes that, although more rigorous research is necessary, there are clear suggestions of such a link.

What, then, can be surmised about the usefulness of existential theory in understanding callings to the Episcopal ministry? At the broadest level the belief that one has been called by God to do his work is a profound statement of one's meaning. What could be more meaningful to a religious person than to become a special conduit of God's grace? Further, from Emmons's perspective the finding of a new meaning to life is an integrating experience. He thus links callings, as spiritual experiences, to personality growth.

When the focus is narrowed to the three pathways found in my interviews with the aspirants, what light does existential theory shed? The group of mostly healthy young adults from supportive, religious families can be understood as incorporating their families' religious value systems. Indeed, callings for these younger persons can be understood as taking their families' religiosity a step further – from a shared belief system to a central aspect of one's personal identity; from "This is what I believe" to "This is who I am."

The second psychological pathway, healing marriages, can also be understood as involving changes in persons' systems of meaning. The most probable hypothesis involves the change from the belief that close connections are inherently dangerous to the belief that psychological intimacy can be safe. To learn this lesson from a human partner then could lead to a closer relationship with God, out of which a calling is experienced.

As indicated earlier in this section, the existential perspective permeates the literature on growth through adversity. Indeed, both finding meaning in the suffering adversity involves and potential changes in one's basic system of meaning are thought by many who study responses to adversity as the primary pathway of recovery and growth. In this sample of aspirants the usual reported consequence was an intensification of a previously held religious belief system leading to or setting the stage for the experience of being called to God's ministry.

Despite the strong intuitive appeal of existential theory as a useful lens through which to better understand the psychology of callings, the systematic studies that have been done all suffer the same flaw: there are no systematic precalling data. As a consequence we must face the question of what to make of calling narratives. This leads to the next section, narrative theory and its implications for an understanding of callings.

Narrative Theory

An offshoot of constructivism (reality is constructed in the mind of the observer and in dialogue with others); narrative theory is, in many ways, the most radical lens through which to view the psychology of callings. What "really" happened is less important than how it is construed and incorporated into one's life story. Further, one's life story is one's identity and is constantly and unknowingly revised. The past is altered to better fit the present and anticipated future – all in the service of maintaining a coherent sense of self, an aid to constructing the belief that life has meaning.

Narrative theory has generated a huge literature and space precludes even a cursory review. Rather, I shall focus on the work of McAdams who I believe presents the most comprehensive theory of narrative identity as well as significant research documenting some of its premises (6,39,75-84).

McAdams suggests that the self can be thought of as the "I" and the "Me." The I is considered as those processes that integrate the self both internally and with the world. The I is the agentic part of the self and is similar to, if not the same as, the psychoanalytic ego. The Me is the product of the I, and McAdams describes three parts to the Me. The first part is the group of dispositional traits – those relatively nonconditional, decontexualized personality traits that have demonstrated genetic roots. This part of the Me is relatively unchanging after early adulthood. Traits provide an excellent first read but not anything like a complete view of the self.

The second element of the Me is called "personal concerns" and includes a wide variety of constructs. McAdams includes motives, defense mechanisms, coping styles, developmental issues, life tasks, attachment styles, and core relationship patterns under the umbrella of personal concerns. Unlike traits, these aspects of the self are contexualized in time, place, and role. Understanding this aspect of the self adds greatly to one's understanding of one's self and the self of others.

The third element of the Me is the life story, the autobiographical narrative one tells oneself and certain others. The life story is considered one's identity. Its function is to provide a coherent, unified sense of who one is and, most importantly, to construct a purpose or meaning for one's life. In the life story past is related to present and both are related to an anticipated future. This approach to identity emphasizes that the life story is constructed and undergoes constant revision throughout the life cycle. It is somewhere between fantasy and "slavish chronicle" (84, p 307).

Life stories are influenced by culture, class, gender, and other shaping influences. They also arise out of prevalent literary traditions and can be judged by their richness, coherence, and creditability. McAdams suggests that midlife narratives of the self often deal with the attempt to reconcile internal contradictions and to develop a generative focus in which self-needs become secondary to the needs of others – including succeeding generations.

Analysis of life stories reveal two recurrent major themes; intimacy and power. Intimacy and power can be measured using a projective test approach. The intimacy motive is defined as a recurrent emphasis on the expression in one's life story of warm, close relationships that are ends rather than means to other ends. The power motive is described as the emphasis on experiences in which one masters the environment and emerges as separate and autonomous. Having impact, feeling strong, and feeling in control are the hallmarks of the power theme.

Life stories also contain a usually small number of turning points. Although there are a number of types of turning points, our purposes here are served by a consideration of two; redemptive and contaminating sequences (39). McAdams defines these as narrative strategies that concern how people make sense of personal experiences that entail significant transformations in affect. Redemption strategies depict a transformation from a bad, affectively negative scene to a good, affectively positive one. "The bad is redeemed, salvaged, mitigated, or made better in light of the ensuing good" (39, p. 474). Contamination strategies involve a transformation from a good, affectively positive scene to a bad, affectively negative one. "The good is spoiled, ruined, contaminated, or undermined by what follows it" (39, p. 474).

McAdams suggests that redemptive and contaminating narrative strategies likely involve both how a person chooses to remember and understand the past and how things actually occurred. Regarding the latter, he offers the qualification that other things likely also occurred and are not remembered.

He also presents a thorough discussion of how ego mechanisms of defense may influence the life story (83). His emphasis is that defense mechanisms can be also thought of as narrative strategies that shape how the life story is told and what it is about. Thus, defense mechanisms are linked to the "tellability" of a life story. Some stories are rendered more tellable by defense mechanisms; others less tellable.

Intellectualization, denial, projection, and other ego defenses are, as a consequence, linked to narrative identity.

McAdams also raises the question of who the life story is intended for – who is the listener? (83). He offers the intriguing idea that the life story is intended for internalized others, thus establishing a connection with psychoanalytic object-relations theory. This brief review of some of McAdams's innovative theory of the self with its emphasis (for present purposes) on narrative identity needs to also involve a sampling of the significant body of systematic research he and his colleagues have accomplished. Once again, however, I will present only a brief review of several of his findings.

First, highly generative adults are more likely than persons of lower generativity to narrate their lives in a commitment story (80, 83). Such a story involves favorable early life circumstances, the early exposure to others' suffering, the development of a stable, compelling ideology, the adoption of goals to benefit society, and the use of redemptive narrative strategies. In contrast to others, these highly generative adults are four times more likely to use redemptive strategies. Persons with lower levels of generativity use twice as many contaminating strategies than do the highly generative. Redemptive strategies are correlated with greater life satisfaction, higher self-esteem, and a greater sense of coherence in life. Contaminating strategies are associated with reduced self-esteem and a greater prevalence of depressive disorders.

The strengths of the intimacy and power themes are associated with gender, marital outcome, and generativity. Generativity is characterized by high levels of both power and intimacy motivation.

Adults over age 40 demonstrate a greater propensity to construct narrative identities that seek harmony and reconciliation of internal contradictions (80). They also demonstrate an increasing concern in their life narratives about issues of generativity – that is, concern about those things, people, and ideas they are going to leave behind.

This brief introduction to McAdams's work or narrative identity does not do justice to the extent of his contribution. It does, hopefully, suggest why it qualifies as a useful lens through which to view adult transformations.

What, then, does the narrative theory of McAdams have to say about callings? First of all, I have not found anything he has written directly about spiritual experiences in general and callings in particular. Despite this observation, there is much in his narrative theory that may speak to the calling experience.

The first issue is the clear suggestion in the aspirants' stories that their callings were turning points that resulted in psychological growth. At least such seems clear in the stories of the middle-aged aspirants whose lives had started in dysfunctional families and involved adult relational failures. Their callings – associated with either a severe crisis or a healing marriage – appear to be clear examples of what McAdams called redemptive narrative strategies. Early childhood abuse/neglect and subsequent relational failures are replaced by a positive resolution of crisis or a healing marriage. The callings to serve God arose in those psychological contexts. The resulting reported changes in the self involved an increased emphasis on intimacy and generativity, considered by most students of adult development to be essential components of psychological maturity. McAdams is clear on the issue of the relationship of narrative construction and psychological growth. He writes, "The process of putting life experience into a meaningful narrative form influences psychological growth, development, coping, and well-being" (84, p. 210). It is the process of narration that leads to both integration of the self and maturity.

Those younger subjects, mostly healthy and from loving, supportive families, do not present life narratives that suggest their callings are redemptive turning points. Rather, these stories suggest continuity. Although sometimes associated with inner struggle, their callings suggest an internalization of family religious values and a continuing healthy development. As noted in an earlier section, however, these younger aspirants have yet to face the midlife developmental challenges of re-appraisal of their lives and life dreams, and it will require longitudinal data to know better their outcomes.

The central problem of the narrative approach to callings is the problem associated more generally with narrative theory. The issue is the relationship of changed life narratives to changed behaviors. At one pole of an interpretive continuum is the premise that if one's narrative identity changes, appropriate changes in behavior (e.g. increased empathy, intimacy, and generativity) will naturally follow. At the opposite pole is the premise that unless changes in behavior can be validated by systematic observations, no claim can be accepted. This more skeptical position might emphasize that reported positive changes represent the demand characteristics of a particular culture. Those called to God's service should be more caring, less self-centered, and the like, and it is this expectation that gets included in the stories of callings.

Further, the skeptics would point out there is good evidence that our past histories are unknowingly rewritten, and how can one rule out that much of the earlier psychological dysfunction has not been created (or exaggerated) in the minds of the subjects in order to document the overcoming of pain and suffering as a central theme of the calling experience?

These dilemmas are not currently resolvable if one accepts the idea that resolution requires systematic observational measures of psychological change and health obtainable only through careful longitudinal studies. Such studies of life narratives do not currently exist. Thus, despite the excitement and promise of narrative theory as a way to better understand callings, we are left with important questions.

Research on Two—Person Relationships

The second focus I have chosen with which to explore the findings from this study of callings is more empirically based than the theoretical constructs discussed above. If one's relationship with God can be considered a two-person interaction, what is known scientifically about two-person relationship systems that are understood to facilitate growth in one or both participants? Can what is known about them shed any light on the psychological aspects of callings?

The two-person relationships that have been most vigorously and systematically studied are the psychotherapy relationship (therapist-patient), the mother-infant relationship, and the marital relationship. The research literature on these three relationships is huge and well beyond the scope of this book. Rather, I will describe briefly a relationship dynamic found in all three and believed to be central to the individual growth that can result. Then the relationship dynamic will be discussed as it may apply to a relationship with God and, in particular, the experience of being called to His ministry.

I have proposed that in the three most intensely studied two person relationships (infant-mother, patient-therapist, and marital), a particular dynamic can be identified (85, 86). This dynamic has three stages; establishment of a strong emotional bond, the temporary rupture of that bond, and the subsequent repair of that rupture. It is the repeated experience of the bond-rupture-repair sequence that underlies and makes safe the internalization of the important other. The reader may find the details of this argument in the original papers:

Here I will only briefly refer to some of the data supporting this growth-promoting dynamic.

The infant-mother relationship has been studied by many developmental researchers. Here only the work of Tronick and his collaborators will be noted. Using slow-motion photography they discovered that most mothers were correctly attuned to their infants' emotional states only about 30 percent of the time (87, 88). Infants, however, signaled in various ways their negative responses to maternal misattunements and the mothers (in another 30 percent of the instances) made an appropriate correction. The bond-rupture-repair sequence was identified.

The psychotherapeutic relationship has also been studied for many decades and by researchers of different theoretical persuasions. Here I will only note several studies of the psychotherapeutic alliance. Horvath and Luborsky, for example, documented that the strength of the established relationship accounted for as much as 50 percent of the outcome. (New insights, increased mastery and the like accounting for the remainder of the outcome) (89). Safran and his colleagues examined the nature of the therapeutic alliance, and, using analyses of verbatim transcripts of therapy sessions, demonstrated that the strongest predictor of positive outcome was the therapist's recognition and correction of his or her misattunements (90). Again, it appears that the bond-rupture-repair dynamic is at play.

Marital researchers have also identified the breakdown in communication resulting from misattunements between the partners, the resulting conflict (about who is right), and the absence of effective repair processes. Those couples who respect each other's subjective reality are most likely to correct misattunements and derail conflict (26, 27). Again, the bond-rupture-repair dynamic can be seen.

If, then, the bond-rupture-repair sequence can be interpreted as underlying the processes of internalizations resulting in new and positive internal representations and their associated personality growth, what can be said about their applicability to callings? Although religious callings can be understood as the formation of a new (or strengthening a pre-existing) bond with God and the resulting establishment of a new and growth-producing internal object representation as an important part of the candidate's revised self, what can be said of misattunements and repairs? This question moves the focus from empirical studies to theology, a discipline far outside my expertise. I found some direction, however, by posing the question of whether the bond-rupture-repair dynamic might apply to a person's relationship with God and a calling to His ministry to a well-informed friend-clinician (91). His response was "process theology and covenant," and he supplied me with an excellent text (92).

Process theology involves the use of contemporary understandings of cognition in recasting God and His relationship with people. It is holistic, dynamic, interactional, and developmental. Covenant is thus understood as "a dynamic and evolving relationship between God and people throughout a historical process" (92, p. 114).

Although commonly thought of in terms of God's relationship with Israel, in its broader sense it is a contractual relationship between two parties in which each party's response is contingent on the other's behavior. Covenant is most often used to describe God's relationship to a corporate body (e.g., Israel), although it can also be used to describe His relationship with a person.

A covenant is described as involving a sequence of interactional phases. The first is that God enters into a relationship (here I shall say with a person) in which He offers certain contingencies. If the person obeys God's laws he shall be rewarded with God's blessing. If, however, God's laws are not followed he will be punished. The second phase is the acceptance of God's offer by the person. The third phase is the person's breaking the covenant through sinfulness followed by God's withdrawal of His blessing. The fourth phase is the person's repentance, and the fifth phase is God's forgiveness and the re-establishment of the blessing.

If these interactional phases are looked at from the viewpoint of the bond-rupture-repair dynamic it is clear that a correspondence is present. The first two phases (the offering of a relationship and its acceptance) is the establishment of a strong bond. The third phase (sinfulness and withdrawal of the blessing) is clearly the rupture of the bond. Phase four, (repentance) and phase five (forgiveness) speak to the repair of the relationship.

If the correspondence to the bond-rupture-repair dynamic established empirically in the infant-mother, patient-therapist, and marital relationship is to be extended to a person's relationship with God, it would involve several other dimensions. One is that the sequence would need to occur repetitively and over a significant period of time.

Another is that such repetitive sequences of bond-rupture-repair would lead to the internalization of God and the establishment of a powerful and loving internal God representation as a core feature of the person's self. Finally, the process could then lead to psychological growth.

Although this extension of the bond-rupture-repair dynamic into the realm of psychological growth through spiritual experiences seems plausible, it does not necessarily explain why only a few experience a calling as part of the spiritual encounter. Once again, it appears that an understanding of callings involves much complexity.

In this discussion I have ranged broadly from diverse psychological theories to more empirically based observations about the processes of psychological growth as they may apply to the growth that appears to be associated (for many) with the experience of being called. As noted in the initial section of this manuscript, the absence of a psychological theory of callings suggests the need for such a wide net. In the final section of this manuscript I will outline what I believe to be the most promising directions for future research and will briefly describe the kind of research paradigm I think will be most productive.

CHAPTER 6

Overview and Future Directions

Developing a cogent psychology of callings is important for both psychology and theology. Psychology needs to understand better those diverse experiences and their underlying processes that can lead to adult growth, particularly those that appear to reverse the adverse consequences of childhood trauma. The current deficit in understanding is particularly striking regarding spiritual experiences that initiate or reflect adult psychological maturation. Ministers, seminary professors, and others involved in evaluating calling experiences may profit also from a clearer understanding of calling narratives.

In examining spiritual experiences as forms of psychological adaptations to developmental challenges, underlying conflicts, needs for personal meaning, fragmented senses of self, and other relevant psychological states, there is no intent to question their theological significance. The subjects for ordination described in this qualitative study believed that their callings came from God. That belief has its own validity within their religious system of meaning. The shift to a psychological interpretive lens is in the service of trying to better understand why this often life-changing experience happens to certain persons in certain life contexts and not to others.

The central findings of this study are twofold. First, there appear to be three different psychological contexts – or, if one pleases, three different narratives – of the calling experience. One, the fortunate-healthy, involves mostly young adults from loving FOO whose psychological development appears healthy and who can be understood as identifying with their parents' religious values and activities. The other two groups, mostly in midlife, describe dysfunctional FOO (often severely so), and frequent adult relationship failures. One of these two group's lives were turned around by the establishment of a healing marriage. Those who described healing marriages seemed clear that the new relationship preceded or was the context in which their callings occurred. The other group's crucial midlife experience was the resolution of a severe crises (most often depression) in which spiritual influences played a prominent role in recovery.

The second central finding is that the calling experiences of the mostly middle-aged subjects with traumatic early life experiences and adult relationship failures – the healing marriage and resolution of crisis groups – appear to be associated with evidence of personality growth. The precise relationship of healing marriages and resolution of crises to callings is not entirely clear in that both adult experiences have been observed to result in growth in the absence of calling experiences. The same issue confounds our understanding of the fortunate-healthy group of mostly young adults. Most children fortunate enough to be born into psychologically healthy families with strong religious values do not experience callings to religious vocations. How can we understand the few who do? One popular idea in family systems theory is that one child is selected (by a parent or the parents) to be the special one, and subtly encouraged to pursue a religious vocation. That type of family projection system flies in the face of these aspirants' descriptions of family support for their autonomous decisions. Perhaps these issues centering about the question of why the calling is experienced is a reasonable starting point for a series of questions that need to be addressed in future research.

The first question involves the role of genetics in the experience of callings. Can it be that the three different pathways to a calling all involve the activation of genes involved in the tendency to have spiritual experiences? Twelve of the 108 subjects had a parent who was a minister; four of these were Episcopal priests. Although identification with a loved parent is likely a part of this high number (11%), a genetic factor cannot be ruled out. One of the subjects was an identical twin and his twin brother was in seminary pursuing ordination in another denomination.

The most solid genetic data we have is from the previously described "Virginia 30,000" study, and I interpret those data as supporting a genetic component to some aspects of spirituality. Whether those aspects of spirituality involve the propensity for self-transcendence remains an open question. Whether genetic influences on spiritual experiences operate indirectly through their impact on other personality characteristics also remains an open question.

It is, however, a reasonably safe assumption (based on more recent neuroscientific research) that the presumed genetic propensity almost certainly involves multiple genes (no single God gene) interacting together to produce the proteins necessary for the growth of brain circuits involved in spiritual experiences and personality growth. There can be no enduring behavioral changes without underlying changes in brain circuitry.

There is also the perplexing issue of what adult experiences may activate the presumed genes involved in spirituality. The findings from this study and Kirkpatrick's work on God as the ultimate secure attachment figure suggest that the crucial adult experiences are relational in nature. The construction of a loving relationship with God or another human involving a strong emotional bond that facilitates the open expression of hopes, fears, internal contradictions, and other felt vulnerabilities seems crucial to the relational experience. I have suggested that the bond→rupture→repair sequences may have special relevance in personality growth through the medium of relationships. In his comprehensive neurobiological-interpersonal theory of human development, Siegel spells out that it is precisely the repetitive experience of reciprocal explorations of each others subjective reality that promotes the growth of those brain circuits involved in personality maturation (93). Although Siegel writes about conversations with important others, it seems to me that the same dynamic may operate in certain forms of prayer. Here, too, vulnerabilities can be expressed, the self more deeply explored, and behavioral options clarified. Such may be more likely with a loving (benevolent) God than with a wrathful (authoritarian) God. I am not aware, however, of psychological research on the various types of prayer in general and those exploring specifically whether the type of prayer used is related to the concept of God held by the person praying.

Whether the language used is the internalizations and internal self and object representations of psychoanalysis, the change in internal working model (from insecure to secure) of attachment theory, or the revision of internal relationship schema of cognitive theory, growth occurs through the medium of relationships. There are other mechanisms of growth, however, and several of them need to be briefly noted.

Vaillant is one developmental researcher who, in addition to internalizations, cites the facilitation of growth through becoming a member of a group that offers both safety and hope (53). All sorts of groups can do this, although I believe that currently there are more persons in Bible study groups than in any other type of group. A.A. is, however, probably the most outstanding example of groups that facilitate growth in some participants through the provision of safety and hope. One of Frank's four characteristics of effective psychotherapy is a facilitating group, and in discussing his work in the previous section I pointed out the important role of group support in the experience of callings.

Another proposed mechanism of change is from existential psychiatry and focuses on the search for or, more likely, the construction of the belief that one's life has purpose, and that purpose is to be found by the elaboration of either an explicit or implicit system of meaning. These belief systems tend to be multifaceted and involve some combination of values from religious sources, relationships with important others, ethical values, work, and personal accomplishments.

Growth may occur as the result of either a major change in one's system of meaning (e.g., religious conversion), or the intensification of a previously held system of meaning (e.g., callings). These changes in systems of meaning are thought to influence behavior as deep cognitive structures from which important behaviors flow.

The midlife phase of adult development is believed to be the time when one's mortality begins to come into consciousness and promotes a reappraisal of one's life including centrally one's system of meaning. Although some respond with vain efforts to deny the existential dread of death in a search to recapture earlier days, more often the reappraisal results in facing the challenge of generativity – how to be less self-preoccupied and more interested in the welfare of others. For those with an existing system of meaning including important religious values, callings can be understood as intensifications of their system of meaning with a core emphasis on the welfare of others. Such a change in systems of meaning would be understood from this perspective as the key dynamic involved in personal growth.

A final mechanism of change is provided by narrative theory and has been discussed in my earlier description of McAdams's work. If personality traits change but little during the adult years and personal concerns (values, defenses, relationship styles, etc) are more likely to change, it is narrative identity (understood as one's basic sense of self) that is more or less constantly modified in order to adapt successfully to current and anticipated contexts. I have earlier commented on the interpretive dilemma of validating (or not needing to do so) changes in narrative identity and McAdams's view that it is in constructing the narrative itself that personality integration and growth are accomplished. What needs emphasis is the nature of the changes in narrative identity that can be presumed to be associated with maturation. One approach is to use those characteristics of the life narratives of persons with demonstrated high levels of emotional health. Maturation of the person might be assumed if his or her life narrative changed in the direction of increased complexity while retaining coherence, increased tolerance for contradictions, ambiguities, and doubts, greater emphasis or relationship themes and less preoccupation with self-interests, and the increasing use of redemptive narrative strategies (searching for positives in negative situations).

Although there are longitudinal studies in which persons' descriptions of earlier life events and relationships often have been found to be very different at different ages, there are, to my knowledge, no longitudinal studies that focus more comprehensively on stability and change in narrative identity. Thus we do not have the kind of needed systematic data on the development of narrative identity over time.

What does need emphasis here, however, is that the life narratives including the calling experience elaborated by these subjects did have – with but few exceptions – those characteristics of the narratives identified as associated with more generative, mature persons. That much appears clear. What is not clear is the matter of change in the narratives and the underlying processes associated with the change. That the reported changes involved three difference contexts – healthy development, healing marriages, and resolution of crises-searcher seems obvious from this study. But, as pointed out above, why callings occurred in such contexts remains mostly conjecture.

These different approaches to understanding psychological growth are all applicable in our attempt to develop a psychology of callings. They all may operate in some persons or each called person may have a relatively idiosyncratic mixture of growth processes associated with his or her calling.

The Future

Although longitudinal studies are a desirable direction in which to better understand the antecedents and consequences of the calling experience, such are notoriously difficult to accomplish. Issues of sample size, representativeness, and retention as well as appropriate measurements are very difficult to accomplish. Funding for this type of a psychological study is very hard to obtain. My strong preference would be for another interview study in which the major focus is the antecedents and consequences of the calling experience rather than what is reported here, that which has been learned in a format that emphasized evaluation of current psychological status. In constructing a more targeted interview format, the findings from this study (the three patterns of antecedents and the evidence suggesting psychological maturation) could be closely attended, but what other modifications might be useful?

Although a desirable major reliance would be on exploratory interviews by experienced clinicians, other measures should be strongly considered. In what follows I will discuss those that appear most promising.

First, it is extremely important to evaluate the calling experiences of those from different denominations. Whether the findings from this study of Episcopal aspirants would also be found in those seeking ordination in other mainline Protestant denominations is more likely than might be the case in those pursuing a ministry in fundamentalist Bible churches. One would also speculate that calls to the Catholic priesthood with its vows of celibacy might involve different psychological factors. The issue of whether and how denominational influences call for different psychological processes is an important one and needs exploration.

Second, there should be a greater emphasis on the subjective experience of a calling. The data from this study indicate that calling narratives can be either relatively simple (as in some of those young adult subjects for whom a religious vocation was the only seriously considered occupation) or very complex (as in many of those middle-aged subjects whose calling appears related psychologically to the struggle to overcome childhood trauma). Clear operational definitions of simple and complex calling narratives could be developed as an aide to better understanding the implications of these different narrative structures.

There is also a need to more closely explore the role of self-transcendence in calling experiences. I have recently described the rehabilitation of oneness in psychiatry and psychology (94). My intent was to call to the attention of clinicians that oneness experiences are not – as we have long thought – necessarily pathologic but in some persons may represent growth experiences. Silverman, a psychologist-psychoanalyst, spent much of his career demonstrating that the subliminal presentation of symbiotic messages resulted in temporary improvement in a wide range of psychological functions, and a more recent meta-analysis of his and others' work documents those findings (95, 96). Thus, there is much to suggest that the capacity for self-transcendence needs more detailed exploration.

It might also be wise to consider using a self-report personality questionnaire such as that of Cloninger's that includes the propensity for self-transcendence. This might offer a check on the interview findings and help identify those subjects high and low on this trait.

In addition to narrative complexity and self-transcendence an effort should be made to free subjects from evaluatory concerns as they might influence their subjectivity. This could be accomplished both by conducting the study after subjects had been approved for ordination (candidate status in the Episcopal Church) and, as indicated above, by removing the study from the context of a psychiatric-psychologic evaluation. The freedom from potential impact on approval for ordination itself could well lead to more openness to discuss idiosyncratic aspects of the calling experience.

There are other aspects of the subjective experience of a calling that could be more exhaustively explored, and the three noted are meant only to emphasize this important topic.

The second topic that needs more careful exploration is the possible role of genetics in the propensity to experience a calling to a religious vocation. Unfortunately, the present stage of scientific know-how in this area is a serious obstacle. Although a recent press report indicated that the first complete genome of his own was presented to a pioneer genetic researcher, the cost is prohibitive and importantly, may not reveal the complexity of the interaction of components of the genome which is likely more determinative than the structure itself. Thus, at a feasibility level this approach to illuminating genetic influences on spiritual experiences generally, self-transcendence propensities, or callings to religious vocations more specifically is simply not available to us.

In the absence of reported data from ongoing genetic studies regarding religious vocations, we are left with the need to explore more fully with subjects their family histories of not only callings but spiritual experiences more generally and, in particular, the prevalence of oneness-type experiences. Since the latter may vary from peak experiences to meditation, to fly-fishing, such explorations need careful consideration in order to include as broad a range as possible.

When the focus is turned to early experiences within the FOO, the exploratory method used in this study resulted in clear distinctions between functional and dysfunctional FOO. There is, however, a special type of interview, the Adult Attachment Interview (AAI) that could offer even more information (97). The AAI is a semistructured interview of about an hour's duration in which the subject's memories of early experiences with each parent are explored. What is unique about this procedure is that the scoring system emphasizes the processes of the subject's narrative rather than a sole reliance on content. There is much that could be said about this intriguing interview and scoring procedure, but here I wish to note only several findings of particular relevance. First, adults who are scored as having a "secure state of mind regarding attachment" are much more likely to have secure attachments with their own children (as measured by the Strange Situation).

There are two types of "secures", "continuous" and "earned". The former type presents an effective narrative process that describes secure attachments with parents from childhood on. This is the pattern I would anticipate in the mostly young adult aspirants described as the fortunate-healthy group. Earned secures present a story of insecure childhood attachments but do so with an effective narrative process. They have been found to have experienced a healing adult relationship and have secure attachments with their own children. This earned secure pattern is what I predict would be found in the mostly middle-aged groups of healing marriages and resolution of crises.

The advantage of using the AAI in a sample of those called to religious vocations is that the scoring system with is emphasis on communication process has been standardized. Although one must be trained in the use of the AAI, it offers a direct test of the three categories of antecedents found in this study.

Another issue involves the distinct advantage of both interviewing the subject's spouse separately and to interview them together. The former offers a needed check on both the antecedents and consequences of the calling experience. The latter involves direct observation of the couple's interactions – particularly if asked to discuss a difference of opinion – and to compare their interactions to those identified in well-functioning couples.

Consideration should also be given to a standardized instrument to measure values (or systems of meaning). I have used the Rokeach Value Survey, a forced-ranking of two groups of values as one part of assessing the relationship of those couples coming for marital therapy. Here, however, I would use it in order to explore whether those called to a religious vocation differ from the established national norms and, if so, in what ways.

Finally, the clear impression growing out of this study of the subject's levels of psychological health might be confirmed by the use of one or more psychological tests. Psychologists differ on which tests best illuminate psychological health, but perhaps an instrument like the Minnesota Multiphasic Personality Inventory (MMPI) might be a suitable choice. As I made clear in Chapter 2 of this book, if I had to choose between interviews and the MMPI the choice would be the former. The use of such tests in a more targeted study would be to confirm the interview data suggesting the psychological health of all but a few subjects.

There is yet another way to explore the psychology of callings, and that is to see how they turn out. Are there identifiable differences between those whose callings appear to flourish over the years and those who do not? Could, for example, there be differences in the outcome of calling experiences among the three groups identified in this study? These and the answers to other relevant questions about the outcome of calling experiences can be a useful lens through which to better understand the psychology of callings.

Keller has written about the reluctance to use the word "calling" in our secular society (98). She argues that "many people experience calling prowling about on the fringes of their lives" (98, p. 230), and such reflects an often difficult to define yearning for something more. The results of this qualitative study of Episcopal aspirants suggest that callings are for some not on the fringe of life but profound and central psychological experiences that may have identifiable antecedents and important maturational consequences. As such callings deserve much greater attention from psychiatrists and psychologists interested in those experiences that facilitate maturation of the personality. It is hoped that what is presented here is an initial step in that direction.

References

1. James, W. (1985). *The Varieties of Religious Experience.* (1ˢᵗ published in 1902), New York: Penguin Books.

2. Bellah, R.N., Madsen, R., Sullivan W.M., Swidler, A., Tipton, S.M. (1985). *Habits of the Heart: Individualism and Commitment in American Life.* Berkeley, CA: University of California Press.

3. Berry, W (2000). *Jayber Crow.* New York: Counterpoint.

4. Baumeister, R.F. (1991). *Meanings of Life.* New York: The Guilford Press.

5. Proctor, M. (2005). *Do You Hear What I Hear?* New York: Penguin Books.

6. McAdams, D., (1993). *The Stories We Live By.* New York: The Guilford Press.

7. Offer, D., Kaiz, M., Howard K.I., Bennett, E.S. (2000). "The Altering of Reported Experiences." J Am Acad Child Adolesc Psychiatry, 39:6, 735-742.

8. Sroufe, L.A., Egeland, B., Carlson, E.A., and Collins, W.A. (2005). *The Development of the Person: The Minnesota Study of Risk and Adaptation From Birth to Adulthood.* New York: The Guilford Press.

9. Parker, G., Hadzi-Pavlovic, D. (1984). "Modification of Levels of Depression in Mother-Bereaved Women by Parental and Marital Relationships". Psychol Med, 14: 125-35.

10. Quinton, D., Rutter, M., Liddle, C. (1984). "Institutional Rearing, Parenting Difficulties and Marital Support". Psychol Med, 14: 107-124.

11. Kaufman, J., Zigler, E. (1987). "Do Abused Children Become Abusive Parents?" Am J of Orthopsychiatry, 57:2, April.

12. Egeland, B., Jacobvitz, D., Sroufe, L. A. (1996). "Breaking the Cycle of Abuse." Child Devel, 59: 1080-1096.

13. Brown, G.W., Harris, T. (1978). *Social Origins of Depression.* London: Free Press.

14. Roy, A. (1981). "Vulnerability Factors and Depression in Men". British J of Psych, 138: 75-77.

15. Laub, J., Sampson, R. (1994). *Crime in the Making.* Cambridge, MA: Harvard University Press.

16. Caspi, A., Elder, G., Jr. (1996) *Relationships Within Families: Marital Influences.* Oxford: Clarendon Press.

17. Paris, J., Braverman, S. (1995). "Successful and Unsuccessful Marriages in Borderline Patients". J of Am Acad of Psychoanalysis, 23:1, 153-166.

18. Pearson, J.L., Cohn, D.A., Cowan, P.A., Cowan, C.P. (1994). "Earned-and Continuous-Security in Adult Attachment: Relation to Depressive Symptomatology and Parenting Style". Devel and Psychopathology, 6: 359-373.

19. Cohn, D.A., Silver, D.H., Cowan, C.P., Cowan, P.A., Pearson, J. (1992). "Working Models of Childhood Attachment and Couple Relationships." J of Family Issues, 13: 432-449

20. Belsky, J., Pensky, E. (1996). "Developmental History, Personality and Family Relationships: Toward an Emergent Family System." In Robert A. Hinde & Joan Stevenson-Hinde (Eds). *Relationships Within Families: Mutual Influences.* New York: Oxford University Press.

21. Levinson, D. (1978). *The Seasons of a Man's Life.* New York: Ballantine Books.

22. Lewis, J.M. (1997). *Marriage as a Search for Healing: Theory, Assessment, and Therapy.* New York: Brunner/Mazel.

23. Lewis, J.M., Beavers, W.R., Gossett, J.T., Phillips, V.A. (1976). *No Single_Thread: Psychological Health in Family Systems.* New York: Brunner/Mazel.

24. Lewis, J.M. (1979). *How's Your Family? A guide to identifying your family's strengths and weaknesses.* New York: Brunner/Mazel.

25. Lewis, J.M. (1989). *The Birth Of The Family: An Empirical Inquiry.* New York: Brunner/Mazel.

26. Lewis, J.M., Gossett, J.T. (1999). *Disarming the Past: How an Intimate Relationship Can Heal Old Wounds.* Phoenix, AZ: Zeig, Tucker & Co.

27. Lewis, J.M. (1996a). "The Transition to Parenthood: I. The Rating of Prenatal Marital Competence." Family Process, 27: 149-165.

28. Lewis, J.M. (1996b). "The Transition to Parenthood: II. Stability and Change in Marital Structure." Family Process, 27: 273-283.

29. Lewis, J.M., Owen, M.T. (1996). "Stability and Change in Family-of-Origin Recollections Over the First Four Years of Parenthood." Family Process, 34: 455-469.

30. Genova, P. (2000). "What Does Suffering Do?" Psychiatric Times, October.

31. Tedeschi, R.G., Clahoun, L.G. (1995). *Trauma and Transformation: Growing in the Aftermath of Suffering.* Thousand Oaks, CA: Sage.

32. Tennen, H., Affleck, G. (1998). "Personality and Transformation in the Face of Adversity." in *Posttraumatic Growth: Positive Changes in the Aftermath of Crises,* in The LEA Series in Personality and Clinical Psychology. Maywah, New Jersey: Erlbaum.

33. Affleck, G.A., Tennen, H. (1996). "Construing Benefits From Adversity: Adaptational Significance and Dispositional Underpinnings." J of Personality, 64:4, 899-922, December.

34. Nolen-Hoebsema, S., Davis, C.G. (2002). "Positive Responses to Loss: Perceiving Benefits and Growth." Handbook of Positive Psychology, 598-606.

35. Park, C.L., Cohen, L.H., Murch, R.L. (1996). "Assessment and Prediction of Stress-Related Growth." J of Personality, 64:1, 71-105, March.

36. McMillen, J.C., Smith, E.M., Fisher, R.H. (1997). "Perceived Benefit and Mental Health After Three Types of Disaster." J Consulting and Clinical Psychology, 65:5, 733-739.

37. Janoff-Bulman, R. (1999). "Rebuilding Shattered Assumptions After Traumatic Life Events: Coping Processes and Outcomes." in *Coping: The Psychology of What Works.* Ed. C.R. Snyder, New York: Oxford University Press.

38. Janoff-Bulman, R. (1992). *Shattered Assumptions: Toward a New Psychology of Trauma.* New York: The Free Press.

39. McAdams, D.P., Reynolds, J., Lewis, M., Patten, A.H., Bowman, P.J. (2001). "When Bad Things Turn Good and Good Things Turn Bad: Sequences of Redemption and Contamination in Life Narrative and Their Relation to Psychosocial Adaptation in Midlife Adults and in Students." Personality and Social Psychology Bulletin, 27:4, 474-485, April.

40. American Piety in the 21st Century: New Insights to the Depth and Complexity of Religion in the US. Selected Findings from the Baylor Religion Survey, September 2006. Conducted by The Baylor Institute for Studies of Religion and Department of Sociology, Baylor University.

41. Weagraff, J.D. (1996). "Second Vocations: A Constructive Developmental Interpretation of the Mid-Life Call to Ministry", U.M.I. Dissertation Services, Ann Arbor, MI.

42. Frank, J.D. (1973, 2nd Ed). *Persuasion and Healing.* Baltimore: The Johns Hopkins University Press.

43. Frank, J.D., Frank, J.B. (1991). *Persuasion and Healing.* Baltimore: The Johns Hopkins University Press.

44. Caspi, A., McClay, J., Moffitt, T.E., et al (2002). "Role of Genotype in the Cycle of Violence in Maltreated Children." Science, 297(5582), 851-854.

45. Caspi, A., Sugden, K., Moffitt, T.E., et al (2003). "Influence of life Stress on Depression: Moderation by a Polymorphism in the 5-HTT Gene." Science, 301(5631), 386-389.

46. Waller, N.G., Kojetin, B.A., Bouchard, Jr., T.H., Lykken, D.T., Tellegen, A, (1990). "Genetic and Environmental Influences on Religious Interests, Attitudes, and Values." Psychological Science, 1:2 March.

47. Joseph, J. (2001). "Separated Twins and the Genetics of Personality Differences: A Critique." Am J of Psychol, 114:1, 1-30, Spring.

48. D'Onofrio, B.M., Eaves, L.J., Murrelle, L., Maes, H.H., Spilka, B. (1999). "Understanding Biological and Social Influences on

Religious Affiliation, Attitudes, and Behaviors: A Behavior Genetic Perspective." J of Personality, 67:6, 953-984, December.

49. d'Aquili, E., Newberg, A.B. (1999). *The Mystical Mind: Probing The Biology of Religious Experience.* Minneapolis, MN: Fortress Press.

50. Cloninger, C.R., Przyeck, T.R., Surakic, D.M. (1991). "The Tridimensional Personality Questionnaire: U.S. Normative Data." Psychological Reports, 69:1047-1057.

51. Comings, D.E., Gonzales, N., Saucier, G., Johnson, J.P., MacMurray, J.P. (2000). "The DRD4 Gene and the Spiritual Transcendence Scale of the Character Temperament Index." Psychiatric Genetics, 10:4, 185-189.

52. Hamer, D. (2004). *The God Gene: How Faith is Hardwired Into Our Genes.* New York: Doubleday.

53. Vaillant, G.E. (1993). *The Wisdom of the Ego.* Cambridge: Harvard Univ. Press.

54. Kernberg, O. (1976). *Object Relations Theory and Clinical Psychoanalysis.* New York: Jason Aronson, Inc.

55. Kohut, H. (1984). *How Does Analysis Cure?* Arnold Goldberg and Paul E. Stepansky (Eds), Chicago: The University of Chicago Press.

56. Rizzuto, A.M. (1979). *The Birth of the Living God: A Psychoanalytic Study.* Chicago: The University of Chicago Press.

57. Howe, L.T. (1995). *The Image of God: A Theology For Pastoral Care and Counseling.* Nashville: Abingdon Press.

58. Bowlby, J. (1969). *Attachment and Loss: Attachment.* New York: Basic Books.

59. Bowlby, J. (1973). *Attachment and Loss: Separation, Anxiety and Anger.* New York: Basic Books.

60. Bowlby, J. (1979). *The Making and Breaking of Affectional Bonds.* London: Tavistock.

61. Ainsworth, M.D.S., Blehar, M.C., Waters, E., and Wall, S. (1978). *Patterns of Attachment: A Psychological Study of the Strange Situation.* New Jersey: Erlbaum.

62. Hazan, C., Shaver, P. (1987). "Romantic Love Conceptualized as an Attachment Process." J of Personality and Social Psychology, 52:3, 511-524.

63. Bartholomew, J. (1990). "Avoidance of Intimacy: An Attachment Perspective." J of Social and Personal Relationships, 7:147-178.

64. Kirkpatrick, L.A., Hazan, C. (1994). "Attachment Styles and Close Relationships: A Four-year Prospective Study." Personal Relationships, 1:123-142.

65. Kirkpatrick, L.A., Shaver, P.R. (1990). "Attachment Theory and Religion: Childhood Attachments, Religious Beliefs, and Conversion." J for the Scientific Study of Religion, 29:3, 315-334.

66. Kirkpatrick, L.A., (1997). "A Longitudinal Study of Changes in Religious Belief and Behavior as a Function of Individual Differences in Adult Attachment Style." J for the Scientific Study of Religion, 36:2, 207-218.

67. Kirkpatrick, L.A., Shaver, P.R. (1992). "An Attachment – Theoretical Approach to Romantic Love and Religious Belief." Personality and Social Psychology Bulletin, 18:3, 266-275.

68. Kirkpatrick, L.A. (1998). "God as a Substitute Attachment Figure: A Longitudinal Study of Adult Attachment Style and Religious Change in College Students." Personality and Social Psychology Bulletin, 24:9, 961-973.

69. Havens, L. L. (1973). *Approaches to the Mind*. Boston: Little, Brown, & Co.

70. Yalom, I. D. (1980). *Existential Psychotherapy*. New York: Basic Books, Inc.

71. Lewis, J.M. (2007). "Do Meanings Matter?" Practicing Column in Psychiatric Times, Vol. XXIV, No. 1, Pg. 25-26, January.

72. Frankl, V.E. (1959). *Man's Search For Meaning*. First published 1946, Boston: Beacon Press.

73. Becker, E. (1973). *The Denial of Death*. New York: The Free Press

74. Emmons, R.A. (1999). *The Psychology of Ultimate Concerns: Motivation and Spirituality in Personality*. New York: The Guilford Press.

75. McAdams, D.P. (1996). *Power, Intimacy, and the Life Story: Personological Inquiries into Identity*. New York: The Guilford Press.

76. McAdams, D.P., de St. Aubin, E., Logan R.L. (1993). "Generativity Among Young, Midlife, and Older Adults." Psychology and Aging, 8:2, 221-230.

77. McAdams, D.P. (1994). "A Psychology of the Stranger." Psychological Inquiry, March, 5:145-148.

78. McAdams, D.P. (1995). "What Do We Know When We Know a Person?" Journal of Personality, 63:3, September, 365-396.

79. McAdams, D.P. (1996). "Personality, Modernity, and the Storied Self: A Contemporary Framework for Studying Persons." Psychological Inquiry, 7:4, 295-231.

80. McAdams, D.P., Diamond, A. de St. Aubin, E., Mansfield, E. (1997)"Stories of Commitment: The Psychosocial Construction of Generative Lives." Journal of Personality and Social Psychology, 72:3, 678-694.

81. McAdams, D.P. (1998). "The Role of Defense in the Life Story." Journal of Personality, 66:6, December 1125-1146.

82. McAdams, D.P. (2001). "The Psychology of Life Stories." Review of General Psychology, 15:2, 100-122.

83. McAdams, D.P. (1993). *The Stories We Live By: Personal Myths and the Making of the Self*. New York: The Guilford Press.

84. McAdams, D.P., Pals, J.L. (2006). "A New Big Five: Fundamental Principles for an Integrative Science of Personality." American Psychologist, 61:3, 204-217.

85. Lewis, J.M. (1998). "For Better or Worse: Interpersonal Relationships and Individual Outcome." Am J Psychiatry, 155:5, 582-589, May.

86. Lewis, J.M. (2000). "Repairing the Bond in Important Relationships: A Dynamic for Personality Maturation." Am J Psychiatry, 157:9, 1375-1378, September.

87. Tronick, E., Als, H., Adamson, L. et al (1978). "The Infant's Response to Entrapment Between Contradictory Messages in Face-to-Face Interactions." J Am Acad Child Psychiatry, 17:1, 1-13.

88. Tronick, E., Gianino, A., (1986). "Interactive Mismatch and Repair: Challenges to the Coping Infant." Zero to Three, 6:3, 1-6.

89. Horvath, H.D., Luborsky, L. (1993). "The Role of the Therapeutic Alliance in Psychotherapy." J Consult Clin Psychology, 61:4, 561-573.

90. Safran, J.D., McMain, S., Crocker, P., Murray, P. (1990). "The Therapeutic Alliance Rupture as a Therapy Event for Empirical Investigation." Psychotherapy, 27:2, 154-165.

91. Davis, C.W. (2007). Personal Communication.

92. Gruse, R.K. (2000). *The Old Testament and Process Theology*. St. Louis, MO: Chalice Press.

93. Siegel, D.J. (1999). *The Developing Mind: Toward a Neurobiology of Interpersonal Experience.* New York: The Guilford Press.

94. Lewis, J.M. (2007). "The Rehabilitation of Oneness." Practicing Column, Psychiatric Times, June.

95. Silverman, L.H. Lachmann, F.M., Melich, R.H. (1982). *The Search for Oneness.* Connecticut: Internat Univ Press.

96. Hardaway, R.A. (1990). "Subliminally Activated Symbiotic Fantasies: Facts and Artifacts." Psychological Bulletin, 107:2, 177-195.

97. Main, M. (1993). "Discourse, Prediction, and Recent Studies in Attachment: Implications for Psychoanalysis." J Am Psychoana Assn, 41:209-244.

98. Keller, R.S. (1995). "Calling Prowls About in Our Lives", Quarterly Review, Fall, 227-236.

ABOUT THE AUTHOR

Dr. Lewis is chairman emeritus of the Timberlawn Psychiatric Research Foundation and clinical professor of psychiatry at the University of Texas Southwestern Medical School. He is also in private practice of individual, marital and family therapies in Dallas.